151

Quick Ideas

to
Get New
Customers

By Jerry R. Wilson, CSP

CAREER
PRESS

Pompton Plains, NJ

151 Quick Ideas to Get New Customers
Edited by Astrid deRidder
Typeset by Christopher Carolei
Cover design by The Visual Group
Printed in the U.S.A.

To order this title, please call toll-free 1-800-CAREER-1 (NJ and Canada: 201-848-0310) to order using VISA or MasterCard, or for further information on books from Career Press.

The Career Press, Inc., 220 West Parkway, Unit 12
Pompton Plains, NJ 07444
www.careerpress.com

Library of Congress Cataloging-in-Publication Data

Wilson, Jerry R., 1944-2005
151 quick ideas to get new customers: attract an endless flow of business at no or little cost / by Jerry R. Wilson.

p. cm.

Includes index.

ISBN 1-56414-830-0 (paper)

1. Relationship marketing. 2. Customer loyalty. I. Title: One hundred fifty-one quick ideas to get new customers. II. Title.

HF5415.55.W54 2006
658.8'12--dc22

2005050849

Contents

Foreword

My company is in the insurance business, and our motto is *In Business To Write Business.* Years of experience have led me to believe that "Nothing happens until someone sells something." This must read book by Jerry Wilson provides you with the prospecting mindset, tools, and techniques you need to successfully prospect for new customers.

Today's prospects are more cynical and skeptical than ever before. They have heard many stories that turned out to be false and been made promises that never came to pass. They have had to become tough minded and demanding, especially when considering new products and services, or selecting new suppliers. This book helps you see the buying process through the eyes of the customer, which helps you become a better salesperson.

You will enjoy reading and applying these 151 Quick Ideas to better understand a prospect's wants and needs, and how to tailor your products and services to fit them. The secret of being *In Business To Write Business* is to convey your value and benefits, which will help you to win new customers.

With these *151 Quick Ideas to Get New Customers,* Jerry arms you with a systematic approach to avoid the stereotypical sales pitches that turn prospects off. You can move away from mass product-oriented marketing, intrusive sales pitches, and cold calling and towards a more efficient method of getting new customers.

You will also learn to maintain Top of Mind Awareness with your prospects and customers. You will discover that "We wouldn't worry about what people think of us if we knew how seldom they do it." This book can be a mandate for action for you and your staff.

I recommend you start by making sure your sales and management teams are prepared with this valuable book. If you are *In Business To Write Business*, then this book is for you. And remember, nothing happens until someone sells something! Good Prospecting!

Roger Looyenga, CEO
Auto-Owners Insurance Company

How to Use This Book

Every quick idea in this book has been selected to directly or indirectly help you gain and retain customers, create relationships, and build a successful business.

Don't try to implement all 151 ideas at once, because some won't be a good fit right now. Read through all 151 quick ideas and select only those that can really make a difference at the moment. Don't worry, you'll go back and review the others periodically.

Label your ideas…

♦ Implement now.

♦ Review again in 30 days.

♦ Pass the idea along to _____.

Involve your staff in selecting and implementing these ideas, and don't forget to give credit for their success! Invest in additional copies of this book and distribute them among your staff. Get everyone involved in selecting and recommending various quick ideas.

Revisit this book every 90 days. As your business changes, you will find new quick ideas that might suit you better now that competition is heating up.

Remember, all the ideas in this book have been proven in businesses across the United States and around the world. They have worked for others and will work for you!

One Thing Worse Than a Rude Employee

Not every person is cut out to help you prospect for new customers. You've been told before and you'll hear it again, hire for attitude and train for aptitude. The people in your business who meet and greet customers have to do it with a smile. Prospecting for customers requires people with a pleasing, positive, and agreeable attitude. Anyone without that mindset needs to leave your business!

When an Illinois farm implement dealership confronted the fact that their parts manager was a walking encyclopedia for tractors, combines, and implement equipment, they also had to admit he was the most cantankerous guy east of the Rocky Mountains. He constantly aggravated fellow employees and drove away customers. They had to debate between the value of his knowledge and his continual conflicts with customers. They finally reached a decision and had to invite him to pursue other employment. Immediately

> ### *Assignment*
> A good prospector evaluates the people who are helping him or her to achieve his or her goals. If you have people who are not willing to work to bring in new customers, you need to evaluate whether they should stay in your business.

after this problem employee left, many prospects returned to the company and became customers. It seems that he had alienated a great number of people over the years, and they had begun to avoid this dealership. Once he was gone however, things changed, and business soon picked up.

> **Epilogue**
> *The only thing worse than allowing a rogue employee to destroy your attempts to get new customers is paying him or her to do it!*

2

Bribe the Significant Other

There's nothing better than selling a prospect, but it doesn't hurt to include their spouse or significant other in your sales effort. In fact, that significant other may become the key motivator to get your prospect to become your customer. After all, it never hurts to have more influence with your prospect.

When a major distributor was planning his sales conference at the Opryland Hotel in Nashville, Tenn., he decided to invite the significant others of his prospects. His company had worked hard to build a database with all their prospect's names, and a special message was sent to their homes. The offer was to come to the conference for an all-expense-paid weekend experience with hors d'oeuvres, good food, a touch of business, and some classy entertainment. Throw in a really deluxe room, a bottle of wine, a gift card to pay for

> **Assignment**
>
> Start now gaining and building a database of your prospects' and customers' partners, family names, and home addresses. In the days and years to come, this list will be as valuable as any you will ever have.

14

incidentals, and some free time to enjoy Opryland, and the entire event became a huge success. It's conceivable that some of the spouses and significant others may have been more sold on the company than the original prospects! Regardless, the event paid off in a big way, and the major distributor earned some major new customers.

Epilogue

You can never have too much influence with a prospect or customer, so use whatever means are available to convince them to join your business. You can often use spouses or partners to give that last extra effort to push your prospect over the edge and become your customer.

3

Involve the Family

If you truly want to build long-term name recognition and convince prospects that you are the best choice, then mailing to their homes can have a huge payoff. Obviously, you need to be careful what you send and make sure it's appropriate to tell and sell your story, but your creativity is endless, so use cartoons, fun newsletters, or contests to involve the family.

When a Virginia-based tire company wanted to better involve both their employees and their prospects in understanding what the company was doing to grow, be successful, and serve its customers, they began mailing a high-quality newsletter to the homes of all prospects and customers in

Assignment

Think about what you can do to involve your prospects' and customers' families. It's a great way, at little or no expense, to tell and sell your story and convert those hard-headed prospects into big buying customers. Let their family help you convince them to join you.

their database. Contained in that newsletter was a code number. Each month they would randomly call two homes, and if the person who answered the phone had read the newsletter and could recite the number, the company would immediately send over two crisp, clean $100 bills. That meant for $400 each month, this company convinced about 1,000 prospects and customers to know about their newsletter, look forward to its arrival, and be involved in the information it provided.

Epilogue

You can't have too much help when it comes to convincing prospects to be your customers. Don't be shy about reaching out to families, because it's a win-win situation for everyone involved.

4

Prospect With a Task Force

Prospecting should be a team effort in your company. The acronym of T-E-A-M stands for Together Everyone Accomplishes More. There's something about the energy, synergy, excitement, enthusiasm, and creativity of getting a group of people working together to win customers that can't be achieved any other way. For this quick idea, our recommendation is that you form a team and call it your prospecting task force.

Each Tuesday morning at 7 a.m., a group of people from different departments gathers at a restaurant to do their prospect planning for the week. The coordinator, their national sales manager, starts the meeting by reviewing their Top 10 prospects from the previous week and the results from their action plan they put together the previous Tuesday. Following that,

> ## *Assignment*
>
> Form a prospecting task force today and follow these ideas and watch what happens. Make sure you pick a diverse group of people from your company for your task force and don't be afraid to move people in and out as you discover how the team works together.

they create a new Top 10 agenda. After that list of 10 is in place, they brainstorm a few action items for the week to come, and assignments are made to various task force members to follow-through. Their real secret is the energy and synergy that flows out of the group. An excellent example of this comes from Ray Kroc, the founder of McDonald's, who said "No one of us is as smart as all of us."

> ### Epilogue
> *Don't wait for something to happen. If you get your task force together today, you can make it happen!*

5

Use Your People

Why do you need to get new customers? Is it because your business is poorly run and you keep losing the ones you have? Are you ready to fill the capacity of your plant, establish a new location, get more volume for economies of scale, or replace the natural attrition that all businesses experience? Hopefully it's because you want your business to grow.

> ### *Assignment*
>
> Examine your sales and workforce. Evaluate their skills and explore educational or training opportunities to increase their skills. Also examine current technologies that can be harnessed to help you sell and create relationships with customers.

If growth is your objective, you might appreciate a reminder of the huge opportunity that educating prospects and customers can produce for you. One of my favorite quotes is, "Your business must grow for people to grow, and people must grow for your business to grow." Think about how the explosion of technology can help you make education a cornerstone of your prospecting efforts. Think about another quote from William Arthur Ward: "The mediocre teacher tells, the good teacher explains, the superior teacher demonstrates, and the great teacher inspires." Remember those words when developing your own educational program. Smart associates make smart decisions, which can help you develop a better business.

> **Epilogue**
> *Examine the finances of any major university, and you will find that their alumni are the driving force behind their success. They have harnessed the power of their former students and their educations. Never overlook the power of education for your employees if you want to enhance your business.*

6

Call Them Associates

One of the awkward things many business owners must decide is what to call their coworkers. Should they be labeled employees, staff, crew, the workforce, or some other descriptive term? My choice, after careful research, is to call them *associates*. If you practice servant-leadership, then you believe that your goal is to create relationships with potential customers. You and your workers are associating together to serve and to help, which makes for a beneficial relationship.

Sam Walton's wife convinced him to use *associates* when the Wal-Mart empire was in its early days and they were starting to be successful, both in growth and market share. She believed that by sharing the bounty, their

> **Assignment**
> This idea could backfire if your employees don't see themselves as associates. You need to address and treat them like associates, with respect and dignity. If you do this, they'll soon see themselves as, and start acting like, true associates.

people would perform and embrace the complete Wal-Mart idea. Did it work? If you've ever been in a Wal-Mart store early in the morning when they have their store meeting and do the Wal-Mart cheer, you know that their associates truly believe in the values and benefits that their company promotes. Many of those associates have since become stock holders, and gone on to become quite wealthy.

Epilogue

Tell me, and I'll forget; show me, and I may remember; but involve me, and I will understand. That is a perfect example of a relationship between associates.

7

If You Want Loyalty

When Cindy's boss saw a pile of new correspondence on his desk, he knew Cindy had been hard at work. On top of the pile was a note that said "If you want loyalty, get a dog. I work for money." In addition to smiling, it got her boss wondering if she was sending him a message. When he asked Cindy about it, she laughed and said "No, I wasn't asking for a raise, although I do work for money. I simply thought you would see it as fun, and might enjoy it." While he enjoyed it, it also

Assignment

Your people are looking for more than just a pat on the back and a thank you. Thank them in a tangible way for the help they've given you, and they'll be quick to help you again tomorrow.

made an impression on him. He realized that sometimes it's important to do more than just say thank you. Employees always appreciate tangible rewards, and loyalty can be rewarded in many different ways.

If you work with one, two, 10, or 100 other people who can help you get new customers, then there are times when it's important to show them your appreciation in a tangible way. It might be as simple as bringing in some doughnuts for everyone, or as important as holding an annual dinner to show your co-workers and associates how much you appreciate their help. In any event, think about giving tangible rewards. You might even consider sharing some of that reward money!

Epilogue

What gets rewarded, gets repeated.

8

Make Me Feel Important

Think back to the last time you had that really warm glow inside when somebody made you feel special because they saw a sign hanging around your neck that said M-M-F-I, or Make Me Feel Important. One of the basic principles of winning customers away from your competition is to make them feel wanted, needed, and appreciated. Every time you see a prospect or customer, mentally

Assignment

Brainstorm what you can do to make people feel important. Develop a system to do it every day, and with every customer.

21

hang that sign around their neck and do something to make them feel important.

Gayle is a regional vice president for a major insurance company. She has grasped the M-M-F-I principle and turned it into one of her tools to gain and retain customers. When she's attempting to get a prospect to represent her insurance company in a particular area, or when she wants to get an existing customer to do something special to benefit her other customers, one of her techniques is to put them on a pedestal by reminding them that they are the best of the best. When she asks them to do something, she makes it clear that she selects the most outstanding people. Rarely does anyone say no, and those who do work with her often develop into loyal customers. Gayle has been able to convert many skeptical prospects into delighted customers by understanding their needs and making them feel important.

Epilogue

Make yourself a note, sign, or poster. Put it on your mirror at home, on your dashboard in the car, or near your phone in the office. Write out M-M-F-I, and remember it every time you contact a customer!

9

Strategic Partnerships

Most companies talk about wanting a relationship with their prospects as they turn them into customers. Unfortunately, many companies often exploit that relationship, taking as much as they can get, even making sales that the customer doesn't need.

Try to be different and see your prospect as a true partner. You should work together to be more profitable and productive.

Mike, a silver-haired and highly successful business owner, left prospecting to his sales force. They had the job to wine and dine prospects until they believed a personal visit from the owner and boss might convince the prospect to come aboard as a customer. Then, when Mike would arrive at the prospect's place of business, he would place a non-descript brown box on the table in the conference room where the meeting would take place. Prospects would always ask what was in the box. He would then remove the lid and show them he had brought a cake, forks, knives, and plates, and that his intention was that they form a partnership that day and celebrate it by cutting the cake, kind of like a quasi-marriage. It was a huge success, and in almost every case the cake, and Mike's presence, would push those prospects over the edge. Mike created and maintained a true partnership with all of his customers.

> ### *Assignment*
> List your customers and prospects. Then identify why you have a good relationship with them, or why you don't. Work to strengthen this relationship until you've created a true marriage of equals.

Epilogue

Prospects don't care about you until they know how much you care about them. Make sure your relationships are positive for everyone. It is important for your prospects to understand that you are not trying to take advantage of them or your relationship.

10

Sell in Bunches

Let's face it, prospecting is hard work, time consuming, and expensive. But it's a necessary evil. Regardless of your feelings about cold calling, prospecting, and constantly looking for new customers, it is a necessary function. You don't have to like it, but you have to do it.

This fall, a local ministry director will invite about 90 church pastors to join him for a free lunch. It will be a no pressure, no selling, no embarrassment agenda on how his ministry can help them grow their church. It will be promoted by a series of three mailings, an e-mail, and a telephone campaign. How many people can pass-up a free lunch?

After the luncheon, this savvy director will encourage the entire audience to self-select by offering a questionnaire about how they might use his services. For those who indicate one or more of the optional services he can provide, he will immediately call on them and work to build a relationship. For those who don't opt for his services, he will at least have met them in person. Now he can start working to build a personal relationship that can eventually turn that prospect into a mission supporter.

> ### Assignment
>
> Always follow the ac-ronym S-A-F-E to make sure people know that it's okay to come to your event. S-A-F-E- stands for Secure, Accepted, Free of Fear, and Enthusiastic. Feeling safe is an incredibly important part of any relationship.

> ### Epilogue
> *The best way to reduce your cost of prospecting and get results is to host a breakfast or lunch during business hours. Pair up a sizzling agenda and a free meal, and you'll be surprised at how quickly your prospects become loyal customers.*

11

People-to-People Prospecting

One quick idea to encourage prospects is to assign an inside person as their direct contact. This can allow you to train those insiders to know a lot about the prospect and be ready if that prospect calls. It gives the prospect a name and a face to connect with, and can be tremendously encouraging to get them to make that first call to your company.

One large car dealership, upon learning about this idea, made a dramatic change in how they approached their prospects and customers. They began using business cards with each person's picture printed on them. They realized they were trying to sell people, not cars. On

Assignment

There are many sources for photo business cards, and with today's digital technology you can send photos to them and have cards back faster than ever. By using digital photography and vendors, affordable and classy cards can be produced, changed, and kept fresh at little or no cost.

the back of each card was a small story about that person, their history with the company, and their commitment to customers. They also printed an 8 1/2" × 11" page with pictures of all their inside customer service people with their names and titles and extension numbers. Now, when you want to call that dealership group, you know more about the person with whom you're dealing. It has been very successful for them, and it will be the same for you.

> ### Epilogue
> *One secret tip is to periodically have customer service representatives and prospects meet face-to-face. It helps to foster personal relationships, which will make it easier to do business together.*

12

Birds of a Feather

One of the most valuable, stimulating, creative, and exciting things you can do is network with other businesses who operate like you, but aren't your direct competitors. Even better is the opportunity to visit other facilities similar to yours and see what different people have used as a business model. It is an opportunity for both parties to learn from their mutual strengths and weaknesses and to benefit from their successes and their failures.

A medical clinic in the Northeast has an unbelievable track record of attracting patients. They have successfully used their system and infrastructure for almost twenty years, but they realize that new ideas similar to theirs could have a huge pay-off. Through a medical association, they were able to identify a dozen other clinics across the United States that are very similar to theirs, but in non-competitive locations. A broadcast letter was sent out to all those on the list and they quickly formed a small group that meets twice a year. They spend two days together reviewing their facilities, talking about their operations, and generally brainstorming about what is working and not working for each of them. It's amazing

> ### Assignment
> Consider putting your own small group together. Get to work identifying other companies like yours and build relationships that can pay off for everyone involved. There are many resources that can help you identify these companies. The secret is to understand that help is out there!

that a group of business people can come together, share their very best ideas, and everyone goes home with new excitement for their business. It's probably one of the biggest payoffs that you can get if you are working on a serious and ongoing prospecting effort.

Epilogue
Yogi Bear, my favorite cartoon character, always said that you can see a lot when you look. Think about how much you can accomplish if you start building relationships with people who have ideas like yours.

27

13

Get Them on Your Own Turf

In developing new customers, it's important to understand how power influences your efforts to convince that customer to do business with you. Any time you're in a customer's place of business or on their turf, you're at a major disadvantage. They have the power and the control to guide and direct what happens. A better idea is to get them on neutral turf, where you can interact as equals. The ideal situation is to get them on your turf, where you can direct the action and capture their complete attention.

> ### Assignment
>
> Remind your sales team about intentional relationships. Discuss techniques to get prospective customers away from their office and onto neutral turf. Then try and explore ideas to bring prospects to your turf, where you are in the power position.

Dave is a master at forging what he terms *intentional relationships* with new customers. One of his strategies is to do everything he can to get a prospect on neutral territory. When Dave has a special offer or a tantalizing deal for a prospect, he invites them to join him for breakfast, coffee, lunch, or an afternoon break so he can have their total attention. When he can, he tries to get them to visit him at his office. This puts Dave in the power position. What are you doing to get your prospects on neutral territory so you can have an equal chance to get them as a new customer?

Epilogue

When you're ready to make that great presentation, invite the prospect to meet you for a meal or coffee to get them out of their familiar environment, and into your sphere of influence.

14

Become a Joiner

Every trade, profession, and occupation has associations that you can join. These trade and professional groups can be a tremendous resource to keep up with changes, network with the most successful people in your trade or profession, and see how other people operate. There are two key secrets to being part of an association: (1) Look at the dues as an investment instead of a cost, and (2) Remember that you have to get involved to get value.

Mae struggled with how to pay employees when some came to work and some didn't during a horrendous snowstorm. She struggled with it until it was time to go to an association meeting. Upon arriving, she found that everyone in her position had anguished over the same problem. She realized she was not alone, and when she

Assignment

Look around to see what local, regional, or national associations you can benefit from. You should handpick a few that you want to get involved with, and contact them about becoming an active member. Remember to R-A-V-E!

left the association meeting that day, she had answers, as well as a list of people she could call when she faced such indecision in the future. To get value out of being a joiner, I use the acronym R-A-V-E. That stands for Read all the materials, Attend the events, Volunteer on projects, and Enjoy the social outlet. There's nothing better to help you learn more than active membership in a good association.

Epilogue

Success is equal parts who you know and who knows you. A good association can help you with both halves of that equation.

15

Intentional Relationships

If you have a spouse, a best friend, or significant other in your life, it is likely that you met by coincidence. But after that first meeting, you made time to build on that relationship. It became an intentional relationship because you created the time and space to get to know each other. The main thing to grasp from this quick idea is the word *intentional*, because it means you made an effort and invested in that relationship. Hopefully all your intentional relationships will be quality investments that pay off.

One of the reasons we talk about giving exceptional service throughout this book is because it is the means to create a positive relationship. If you concentrate on building intentional relationships, you will be creating business, which translates to increased profits for you. But before you can do that, you have to do the things you promise, and demonstrate outstanding service. Then you can turn that prospect into a customer, all because you developed an intentional relationship.

> **Assignment**
>
> Make *intentional* part of your vocabulary to describe the relationships you want to have now and in the future.

> **Epilogue**
>
> *Have you ever wondered how often chance or coincidence was actually guiding you? Chance can open many doors, but you can only walk through them with the right intentions. Intentional relationships take time and effort, but they are definitely worth it!*

16

Are You New or Recycled?

New customers want to be fussed over. They want to feel special. They want to be recognized, accepted, and appreciated for bringing their business to you. But new customers are not more important than old customers, and it's important to remember to appreciate them both. What you need is a system to recognize both those recycled customers who have returned, as well as identifying and rewarding new people who have come aboard for the first time. The key is to put a system in place to make that happen every day with every customer.

A group of California bowling alleys developed a system to serve both customers who were returning, and prospects who were coming in for the first time. They found a very simple way to separate the two groups to reward both of them properly. They asked a simple question: "Have you bowled with us before?" If you said yes, a manager would stop by while you were bowling, and thank you for coming in again. He would also give you a few coupons good for your next visit. If you said you were there for the first time, you were handed a simple brochure that identified a few key things you would want to know about what made their bowling lanes different. The manager would also make sure to stop by while you were there, and he would thank you for coming in. He would even give you a coupon to get free beverages while you were there, as well as a coupon to come back a second time. So they were recognizing and rewarding their customers, which is the ideal situation for you. What are you doing to identify your new customers, while still rewarding the old?

> **Assignment**
>
> Design a key question to ask customers to sort out the new from the returning, and set up a database to track them. Then devise a simple yet effective method to consistently reward both your old and new customers.

Epilogue

Everyone wants to feel special, so make sure your customers know how much they mean to you. Customers will go where they feel invited, and return where they feel appreciated.

17

Love That Loyalty

Part of searching for new customers is occasionally encountering those who hold you at arm's length because of their loyalty to a current supplier. Inevitably they will tell you stories about how their current vendors have gone the extra mile for them. Our instinct, when attempting to get business, is to be defensive and try to overcome that statement of loyalty. That's exactly the wrong thing to do and will do nothing more than alienate that prospect, which means that it's unlikely you will ever get their business. There is a better way to approach the situation.

The first thing to do when someone describes his or her loyalty is to compliment them. If you really think about it, it is a good character trait. Wouldn't you like all of your customers to be so loyal that they throw all your competition out the door? Second, explain to them that loyalty is a

> ### *Assignment*
> Value that loyalty, and tell them so. Then keep right on pitching. At some point, their needs will change or their current supplier will fail them. You want to be there for them when that happens.

rare commodity, and is all too often missing in business today. That's the commonly held perception, even though there are more loyal people out there than we recognize.

Epilogue

Remember, loyalty comes from customer delight. If you do it, they'll want it. Make sure you are ready to catch them when they fall, and you'll have a new loyal customer.

18

Develop a Clear Vision of Success

Several psychologists, motivational experts, and various authors have posited that you can become the vision that you have of yourself in your mind. This is often called visualizing, and is a tool that can help you achieve great success.

> **Assignment**
>
> Adopt the visioning principle. Create a vision for your company and write it down. Create posters, brief everyone in the company, put it on your answering machine or voice mail, and tag it to your letterhead. Surround yourself in your vision of success.

James Allen, the highly respected author of the book *As a Man Thinketh*, says that our mission is to develop a picture in our mind that will lead us to success. For example, picture a prospect as your customer. Picture them in your mind joining you for strategy sessions and filling out big orders. Picture them going to lunch with you wearing your logo jacket. Picture them on the golf course playing the back nine with you. See them on your next fishing trip. This vision of success is particularly useful when talking to prospects. As you develop that picture in your mind, you will subconsciously work harder to realize your goals.

> **Epilogue**
> *If you think you can, you can! Conversely, if you think you can't, you're absolutely correct!*

19

Heroic Tales

Everyone loves stories of heroes. Heroic stories about how you and your crew have gone above and beyond the call of duty in serving your customers can be an awesome sales tool to convince prospects to become your customers. Collect and practice telling your own hero stories because they carry more weight than all the advertising and promotion you could buy.

When Marie arrived to pick up a moving trailer, she was shocked to learn the shop that was supposed to hitch the trailer to her SUV was closing for the day. Marie had rushed there after work and thought they were open for another hour. But there had been a mistake in the shops hours. The owner and one worker were still on hand when she pleaded her case that she was supposed to drive her son (and all his stuff) to college registration the next morning. Without the trailer, she could not move all his furniture and personal items he would need for the next year. As the business owner heard Marie's story, he told her to pull her SUV in and he and his associate would stay and get the trailer wired and ready for her to

Assignment

Don't overlook the power to use those heroic stories for your benefit. They should be happening in your company, so be sure to look for them!

go. He explained he was sorry for the misunderstanding over the hours and his real concern was helping Marie resolve her dilemma. The business owner liked to tell Marie's story to his other customers, both because it made his business look good, and it reminded his staff that heroic deeds could and should be done every day.

When the owner isn't around, do you think this story will remind his employees that they may want to do their own heroics to save and serve customers? This story could pay off for the owner for years to come!

Epilogue

The power of storytelling is both underused and more powerful than most prospectors will give it credit for. You should become good at telling the tales of your own heroics.

20

Do You See What I See?

When I think about my favorite cartoon character, Yogi Bear, I always think of his favorite saying: "You can see a lot when you look." It's time to stop and look around your company to see how you're doing. Ray Kroc and Walt Disney both believed that you should never see a facility, building, vehicle, or anything their company owns that appeared to need cleaning, fixing, or painting. They believed if you do those things routinely, your customers will always see a bright and shiny company that's up to speed.

Assignment

Make it a habit every 30 days to take a walk around your company and look at it through the eyes of your customer.

When Sparkle Pools decided to do an extreme makeover, they found their consultant sitting on a stump across the street from their business. When Tom, Sparkle Pool's owner, went over to inquire what he was doing, he said he was looking at the company as customers see it when they drive in. The exterior of the building needed a coat of paint and one of their signs had faded and was hardly visible. Weeds had grown and the parking lot needed a fresh seal coating. Overall, the business had been allowed to deteriorate and needed to be cleaned, swept, scrubbed, and painted. Think about the message that something like a badly painted wall, or a handrailing that wobbles, sends to your prospects and customers.

Epilogue

Adopt the philosophy of Ray Kroc and Walt Disney that people will never see your business when it needs to be cleaned, painted, scrubbed, or fixed. Remember the power of first impressions!

21

Zero Defections

The best new customers are ones you already have. While some customer attrition is inevitable because customers move away, sell out, go bankrupt, or have other situations that you can't control, you should never accept a lost customer. Accept what you can't change, but never accept losses that are within your control.

George, a seasoned and highly successful national sales manager, claims much of his track record is due to his hating to lose. When it comes to customers, his goal is to have zero defections. He'll never lose a customer he values and wants to keep. When that rare event does happen, George launches his Operation Rescue and makes an all-out effort to regain their

> **Assignment**
>
> Be a private investigator and learn from your lost customers. Don't just accept the loss! Work like crazy to get them back. Remember, you once had a relationship with them, so go back and review what was successful in the past.

business. George believes that to regain lost customers, he's got to become a private investigator, because he wants to learn why a customer might leave him in the first place. Those reasons become valuable lessons to improve all his customer relationships, even if he loses the customer from whom he learned the lesson.

Epilogue

Accepting customer attrition without trying to stem the tide can start a downward spiral. Learn to fight back, and renew those relationships!

22

Turning Off Your Prospects

Like it or not, you're really in the people business. You just happen to offer the products and services that you do. If you can organize, inspire, and energize a group of effective employees, the world is your oyster. It is your guaranteed key to success, regardless of the products and services you offer.

One thing that has leaked out of our *Customerology* research is that prospects and customers hate to see changing faces. They develop friendships, relationships, and get to know people on whom they can depend. Personnel turnover, or churn, is very demoralizing for them. Prospects and customers accept the fact that people get moved, promoted, or transferred, but they hate to hear that they quit or were fired.

Assignment

Before dismissing an employee, ask yourself what impact it's likely to have on your customers. Consider transferring that person to another location and then, when the time is right, exiting them out the door. That way your customers can accept the fact that they moved on normally.

Epilogue

Remember what turns prospects off. An ever-changing personnel roster can be the kiss of death.

23

Pushy Prospectors

A high-impact sales training seminar started by having each attendee place a hand up against the hand of a partner sitting next to them. Then the instructor gave them a command to push. What happened when each person pushed against the hand of the person sitting next to them? Their opponent pushed back. No one likes to be pushed. They love someone who will help them buy, but they'll really dislike someone who pushes

Assignment

You need to become a super-sleuth. Ask, ask, and ask some more, and you will find those hot buttons that trigger a customer's buying cycle.

them to buy, which they equate with pressure.

One prospector completely changed the way he approached getting new customers when he saw a quote that said "The secret is to get other people to do what you want done, because they want to do it." Start today with the mentality of finding a need and filling it, finding a problem and solving it, or finding an opportunity and taking advantage of it. This will help both you and your customer to go from good to great!

Epilogue

Always remember that people hate someone who tries to sell them something, but will love you if you help them buy.

24

Don't Let the Fish Flop Away

When a prospect finally requests something from you, such as a sales catalogue or price quote, you want to put them on your stringer before they can get back in the water. Don't waste time, during which buyer's remorse can set in and the prospect changes his or her mind, or a competitor beats you to the opportunity. Nothing is worse than finally catching a fish, getting him up on the bank, and then watching him slide back down into the water. You need to move quickly when a customer says yes.

When a salesman finally got a prospect to request information on a large wall cabinet full of electrical terminals, he was excited. He promised the prospect that he would be back the next week with the information, pricing, and availability. When he walked in the next week, he nearly had a heart attack as there sat a big display of elec-

> ### *Assignment*
>
> Make certain that when a potential customer says yes, you put that customer at the top of your list and service him or her until you get the sale. Focus your attention on that prospect until you make the deal.

trical terminals this prospect had purchased from another sales rep who beat him to the punch. He learned an important lesson: when a customer says yes, it's time to seal the deal and put him on the stringer. It's time to move fast.

Epilogue

When opportunity knocks, some people complain about the noise, while others spring into action. Which kind of person are you?

25

Your Way or My Way

At one time, K-Mart was the dominant retailer in America. Before they lost their way (and ended up bankrupt and purchased at a sales price by Sears) they had passed Target, JC Penney, and many other retailers at being the biggest and best.

> ### *Assignment*
>
> Think about how you are adapting to serve your customers, not how you are forcing customers to adopt your system.

What was their secret to get new customers? They built a system that was customer-friendly.

Herb Wardlow was the architect who for more than 10 years guided K-Mart as its president. He describes his secret to getting new business as being incredibly simple. Here is the formula: "Find out what your customers want and give it to them...and then some." It's building a system to accommodate your customers' wants and needs, and then doing the many little extra things that will get even more customers to come to you. If you do things their way, you are guaranteed to have delighted customers.

Epilogue

Find out what your customers want and arrange your store and services to suit their needs.

26

Help, Don't Sell

What is the mentality of a salesperson? To get that answer, think about telemarketers who've called you, particularly during the evening. What did you do? Engage them in conversation, or hang up? Most people hate telemarketers because of the intrusion factor. Selling has a bad image. Therefore, you must learn to be a helper, not a seller. Find out what customers' problems are and solve them, and they will see you as someone who is truly committed to helping them, rather than someone who is desperate to make a sale.

To say that purchasing agents are frustrated would be the understatement of a lifetime. Everyone who

> **Assignment**
>
> Make a card that says *Help Before You Sell*. Post it prominently around your office or desk as a reminder.

comes through their door has one thing in mind: to get their business. If you want to be different, find out what their problems are. Find out what frustrates them. Find out what their competitors are not doing. Be seen as a helper, not a seller, and provide solutions. Watch what happens, and you'll be amazed at all your new business!

> **Epilogue**
> *Help comes before sell in what you're doing, as well as in the dictionary!*

27

The Power of Compliments

When was the last time someone gave you a sincere and meaningful compliment, something you knew was from his or her heart and that made you glow inside? If your answer is like the hundreds of people I've asked that question of, all too many of them have turned to me and said "The last compliment? What year is this?" Have you ever met someone who complained about getting too many compliments, or being fussed over too much?

It was hard for people to figure out why they liked playing golf with Harry. While he was an average golfer, there was something he did that drew people to him, wanting to play golf. Finally, one of his colleagues figured it out. When you hit a good golf shot, he would brag about you. He'd say "Boy, you're really going to like that shot. What a great shot." When you sliced one, took a Mulligan, or heard the ball go plop in the water, he'd say "You know what? That's what I seem to do all the time." He could minimize your mistakes, and maximize your successes. In a world that is waiting to criticize you, a compliment has incredible power. You should always find a way to give every prospect one compliment every time you talk with them.

> ### Assignment
> Write down 10 customer names, and then write down one thing you could do to compliment them. Put a smiley-face everywhere you look as a reminder that giving compliments makes people glow inside.

Epilogue
Beware when giving compliments to make sure they are sincere. People instantly know the difference between saccharine and sugar.

28

Become a Yes Person

Customers are in a hurry. Have you ever noticed how the post office capitalizes on that? For an additional charge, they will speed things up. If you want to send a large envelope in three to five days, you're probably going to spend about 50 cents. If you need it there in two days, it will go priority mail and it will cost you around four dollars. If you just can't wait, they'll send it overnight, and you can expect to pay about fifteen dollars. What's the difference? It's the sense of urgency. Can you do the same thing? Do you have opportunities where you could get their work done faster for a small additional charge? Could you stop your normal processes and do it on a special needs basis? More and more businesses are earning and justifying a priority charge for extra service. For example, your dry cleaner, printer, delivery service, clothing alterations shop, and caterer all have two price schedules, a regular and an express.

One Memphis electrical motor manufacturer solved an urgency problem that was constantly interrupting his production line work by adding a same-day charge of 25 percent extra. He quickly found that customers didn't mind paying the additional charge if they really needed their item quickly, but dropped their demands if it wasn't re-

Assignment

Where could you take advantage of offering something better, quicker, and faster for an additional charge? In one manager's office there's a sign that says, "Good, fast, and cheap. Pick any two."

ally necessary. His competitors refused to offer that kind of service. By developing two service schedules, he soon resolved his production line problem. In addition, it earned him a lot of new customers who not only came to him for their emergency work, but began going to him for their regular needs as well.

Epilogue
Customers want options, and even at a slightly higher cost, they will probably welcome the opportunity to get the service and delivery they really want.

29

Sell Your People First

It is amazing how dangerous many business owners and managers are when they hire someone, give them little or no orientation or training, and then simply throw them out on the job. If your people aren't sold on you, your company, and your products or services, how are they going to translate that to your prospects? Training your people must be your first priority if you truly want to convince prospects to come aboard.

> **Assignment**
>
> Make it a rule that every new person joining your organization should go through a procedure to get them indoctrinated in the values and beliefs of your company. Make yourself a checklist of the things they need to know and believe before you let them interact with prospects or customers. Create a training session that trains them with your philosophies and traditions.

Chicago-based Quill Corporation has a rule that new employees can't touch a telephone until they have been through several phases of Quill Corporation training. They learn about the history of the company. They learn about their culture, their rules, their policies, their procedures, and their traditions. They must be able to demonstrate that they are convinced Quill is a great operation before they ever go near a phone. The management at Quill quickly says that they are not about to let an unarmed employee pick up a phone and talk to a prospect or customer when they themselves don't know about or believe in their company.

Epilogue

Prospects don't care how much you know until they know how much you care. If you really care, you'll transfer that to your associates and train your employees to believe in delightful customer service.

30

Fix the Problem

If you've ever called on a potential customer and unknowingly walked into a hornet's nest, you know how critical it is to defuse the difficult situations. A small dose of training can cure a large case of unhappiness. It can also help you avoid an argument that you will rarely, if ever, win.

Fortunately, when Brian got blindsided by a mad engineer, he knew how to harmonize with the complainer. After Brian assessed the problem that had upset the engineer, he asked an important question: "What can we do to fix this problem and make you happy?" By avoiding a confrontation with the customer in which both parties become defensive, he was able to get to the root of

> **Assignment**
>
> Learn how to defuse an angry customer. The key phrase is: *What can we do to fix the problem?* Remember that if your customer is not satisfied with the solution, you could easily lose that customer. It's not a pride issue, so be sure to keep your ego out of your responses.

the problem and resolve it, and turn an unhappy complainer into a happy customer.

> ### Epilogue
> *You may win the argument, but you could lose the customer. Do you want to be right, or have the business?*

31

People Are Funny

Art Linkletter hosted a hit TV show called *People Are Funny*. Prospective customers are also funny, as well as prejudiced, predictable, and picky. Especially when it comes to the appearance of the people with whom they do business. Your appearance can turn them on, turn them off, or even permanently shut down your chances.

> **Assignment**
>
> Learn how your customers want you to look and dress. Develop a standard that fits with their vision, and remain consistent.

Before you grow a beard, get a tattoo, or let your hair grow out, take inventory of how your prospects might feel and react to your appearance. Why start campaigning for new business by turning your prospects off before you ever get a chance to establish a relationship with them? Is this a blinding flash of the obvious to you? Never underestimate the power of appearance. You should do your research, and conform to the expectations of your customers in terms of your appearance.

Epilogue

People want to do business with people who are like them. But they avoid doing business with people who are not!

32

Inspiring a New Hire

When making a job offer, every applicant wants to know about salary. Good employers understand that in addition to answering that question, it is inspiring to brief new hires about when they can expect future pay reviews. For example, a new delivery driver might be told he or she would have a pay review in 90 days, and again at 6 months.

When Chris hired new folks to help him win new customers, he knew their attitude, work ethic, and dependability were musts in his organization. When a new worker got off to a running start and Chris got outstanding feedback about her work, he used a powerful strategy to inspire, and to ensure the new hire would stay with him. At 30 days Chris called her to say that all her co-workers were bragging about her performance.

> ### Assignment
> Make certain you set specific pay review intervals for your sales force so they know what to expect. Accelerate the raise scale for your most successful employees.

Then he reinforced the key behaviors he needed from her. "Judy, you have exceeded our expectations for a new person on the team. Therefore, I am going to exceed your expectations by

49

giving you your 50 cent per hour raise today instead of in 90 days. Then we will be reviewing your pay again in six months." Chris understood that while praise is nice, it doesn't buy groceries! Do you think Judy, the new hire, will do back flips for Chris in the future? You can be sure of it.

Epilogue

An old proverb says "When you drink the water, don't forget to take care of the people who helped you dig the well." By recognizing your successful associates, you will inspire them to work even harder in the future.

33

Respect Their Time

We live in an age where people feel incredible pressure to get things done immediately, both in their business and personal lives. They are trying to accomplish more in less time, and feeling pressured to cram 48 hours worth of activity into a 24 hour day. You can send a huge message to prospects by consistently showing them that you and your company have a sense of urgency about meeting their needs, and that your organization will hustle to serve them.

While standing in line at the local post office, one waiting patron commented

---

Assignment

Identify the key areas in your company where a sense of urgency is important, and show it to your prospects and customers every day.

---

to another, "I'm always amazed that they only have two lines open when they have so many customers, and both of the clerks on the counter seem to be in slow motion. Their demeanor, their body language, and the excessive time they're taking with customer conversations tells me that they really don't care." While I'm sure the post office has some very competent and capable employees who understand their customer's needs, as a whole they've been labeled as having poor customer service because all too often, that's what they provide. Don't allow your company to be like the post office. Develop a sense of urgency that reflects your customers needs.

Epilogue

Your prospects are watching you, and nothing can be more powerful than proving you have a sense of urgency about serving them.

34

Targeting Your Prospect's Interests

The old saying, *Different strokes for different folks*, is certainly true of your prospects. Each will have their individual interests, hobbies, or passions. Your goal is to learn what those are, such as fishing, hunting, golf, collecting antiques, doing woodwork, restoring a house, or building vintage cars. The secret is to know what interests your prospects, so you can become interested in the same thing. When you know what flips a prospect's switch, you can become a 24-hour-a-day research

Assignment

Keep an inventory of notes and a list of what interests your customers, and be looking for those items every day. It can be anything, from an article in the newspaper to a special television show, from a brochure on a new product to an advertisement about a new service.

person looking for something interesting you might pass along to them on that subject.

When one salesperson learned that her customer had just gotten a new puppy, she zoomed right in on that subject. She stopped by a local pet store and found a free quarterly newspaper chock-full of ideas, stories, ads, and articles on the training, nutrition, and care of puppies. She wrote a quick note to her prospect and sent the materials along in the mail. On the next call to that customer, they had a subject to talk about. The customer was so impressed that she took that kind of interest in him, that he soon became one of her most loyal customers.

Epilogue

Prospects are flattered when you recognize and share in their interests, hobbies, or passions. Capitalize on your common ground, and use it to build a personal relationship.

35

All Buyers Are Liars

A group of prospects were meeting with a sales representative at a Colorado steakhouse, and all were complaining that their steaks were overcooked. When the waiter came and asked whether everything was okay, all the people who had just complained said "Sure, everything's fine." As the waiter walked away, one fellow said "I wouldn't come back to this place again if they paid me." How many times have you lied to a waiter or waitress and told them everything was okay, when in fact the service or meal wasn't good? It's easy to remember that there are two kinds of objections that customers have: (1) the ones they tell you, and (2) their real objections.

Ben was a loyal buyer from a warehouse distributor. One day something went wrong, and he stopped doing business with them. He went from being a customer back to being a prospect. When a new sales rep was assigned to call on Ben, he knew that getting the truth about what happened might be difficult. When he sat across from Ben in the office, he asked one

> ### *Assignment*
> Remember the question, "What can we do to earn your business," or "What can we do to get your business back?" When you put the prospect in a situation of helping rather than whining and complaining, the likelihood is they will tell you the truth instead of putting you off.

simple question, "What will it take to win back your business?" He put Ben in a situation where he could be positive and actually share what the business needed to do to get back in his good graces. Instead of allowing Ben to criticize his company, the sales rep allowed Ben to help find a solution.

Epilogue

Great salespeople know it isn't what happens to you, but how you respond to what happens to you that will make your prospecting efforts a success.

36

Brag, Brag, and Brag Some More

Will Rogers said "Get someone else to blow your horn, and the sound will carry twice as far." If you have associates with whom you work who are exceptional at their jobs, it can be a tremendous asset when you're trying to convince customers to join you. From a newspaper ad that features their picture and a story about them, to your personal tribute and stories when you're making sales calls, there are many ways to highlight quality people to help you get new customers. It's a powerful tool.

> ### Assignment
> Identify your top people and the three qualities that make them outstanding so you can tell their story in print, in marketing, and in person.

Jack wasn't just a good machinist when it came to building high-performance engines, he was a great machinist! Many people labeled him a quality fanatic or called him obsessed with the shop's reputation. His reputation was awesome, and the amount of work in his shop showed it. Think about how you could turn Jack's reputation into a sales tool. Think about how you could make that person in your organization bigger than life. People want to be around successful people, and you can take advantage of the successful reputations in your organization.

Epilogue

Sometimes a person's reputation is as valuable as the person themselves. Find out who the stars are in your company, and make sure to highlight their talents and skills.

37

Pay Attention to Their Individual Needs

Customers are people, too! If you pay attention to their needs in addition to offering your products and services, you can benefit a great deal. Like it or not, your business is probably not that much different from your competitors, and you need to recognize that. By making a concerted effort to address each prospect's individual needs, they will be able to find you in the crowd. Capitalize on the features that you make you different.

The owner of a beauty salon was hurting in his attempt to build a customer following. He had many competitors in the area, and

Assignment

Teach everyone your plan to meet the customer's emotional needs, which can be remembered with the easy formula of EN1 = Emotional Needs First.

the simple fact was that they offered many of the same services. He began to recognize the individual needs of his customers with a program to get each person comfortably settled. He made sure they knew what their schedule was going to be and who was going to work with them. Then they were offered a choice of beverages and snacks. At the end of each visit, he would have a small gift for the customer to take home, and he always made sure to tell his customers how important they were, and remind them to come back again.

Epilogue
It's one thing to tell people that you care and they matter. But it is 1,000 times more important to show them you care, and they really do matter.

38

My Name's Not Bud

How serious are you about attracting new customers and cultivating long-term relationships with repeat buyers? If that's your intention, beware of the tragic blunder many companies have made in trying to win my business. I've been called bud, chief, sweetie, honey, honey-pie, lover, and everything except my actual name. While this may seem trivial to many, psychologists say that a person's name is, to them, the sweetest sound. Start by making sure that your associates have their name available so your prospects and customers can use their name, and begin building a relationship.

Membership retailer Sam's Club is currently running a campaign about using customer names. On the back of every cash register, you will see the word C-H-A-N-T. That is a reminder to all Sam's employees that Customers Have A Name, Too. In fact, they run rewards to remind employees of the importance of identifying people by their names. Do you think you can get better at doing that, Bud?

Assignment

Getting and using people's names is a habit. First we make our habits, then our habits make us. Get your associates into the habit of using proper names instead of nicknames.

Epilogue

Getting and using customer names is a very simple tactic that your competition might overlook. Customers in survey after survey complain about being treated like a number, so make sure that your company doesn't do that.

39

Beware of Agitators

There are a lot of great, friendly, and fun people to do business with in America, but for some reason there also seems to be a small group that delights in agitating, debating, and instigating trouble at every step. It seems their life goal is to push your buttons, belittle your company, find faults with your products and services, and tell you that your competitors are better than you. The secret is not to let these people get to you. After

> **Assignment**
>
> Get a book about dealing with difficult people. Read it, and teach the techniques to your staff.

all, if you don't want them to get your goat, don't let them know where it's tied.

The best time to deal with agitators is before you encounter them. Start by making a decision that you are not going to react instinctively. Instead you're going to prepare and respond to those doom and gloom people. Learn to harmonize with their objections, and tell them you can understand their feelings. When they know how to push your buttons, they'll just continue to do it. If they don't know what sends you into orbit, then they'll give up and stop agitating you and pick on someone else.

Epilogue

Don't let the critical few destroy your attitude about dealing with the majority, of whom many are a pleasure to serve.

40

Label What Differentiates You

We live in a world where every business yells and screams, "We are different. We are better. Choose us." In reality, it's usually nothing more than old wine in new bottles. You need to commit to truly being different with a program that prospects can see. Then you must label what you do. The label is a daily reminder, sending a message to prospects, customers, and employees. Marketing professionals call it the *value statement*. You might recognize it as a tag line.

A company called Image One wanted to define their uniqueness, so they came up with the rather clever tag line of *The Image One Way, The Only Way.* This helps their prospects and customers identify their values and ideals. The company now needs to educate their staff about their new tag line, and make sure that everyone understands the philosophy it entails.

> **Assignment**
>
> Define your value statement so that your employees can internalize what you want them to know. Label as many things as you can with it, like your letterhead, pens, or posters. This should serve as a daily reminder to capitalize on what makes you unique!

> **Epilogue**
> *You have to name it to claim it, so decide what makes you unique and slap a label on it. A copyright can help too!*

41

Do Something Different

Prospects just love to be wined, dined, and solicited by potential suppliers, because it means they have been accepted and are valued. Acceptance is one of the key motivating factors in life, but in many areas of customer service, it's no longer enough. You have to do something different, bold, and creative to show your customers that they are valued and accepted. Find something unique, fun, and/or mysterious to convince your

> **Assignment**
>
> Put your own creativity to work developing fun, interesting, and unique ideas to involve your prospects and customers. Organize a team to help come up with some good ideas for special events.

prospects to become your customers.

Vicky was an award-winning sales manager. When she identified her Top 10 prospects and invited them to a very unique customer presentation, each prospect received a series of three mailings inviting them to join her on the dock at a local reservoir to take a leisurely tour on her boat. Hors d'oeuvres, drinks, and a bit of fun were built into the event. The creative mailings went on to explain that ties would be cut off at the neck and anyone not wearing shorts might be thrown into the water. At the appointed hour Vicky was amazed as all 10 prospects were standing on the dock and climbed onto the barge to spend the afternoon schmoozing and learning about Vicky's products. Within weeks, all but two became customers.

> **Epilogue**
> *Most business prospectors are about as exciting as a bucket of warm spit. You need to break through the usual business to convince your prospects to become your customers.*

42

Be Creative

Your competition can be very predictable. They will probably do what they've always done. Very few people are really creative enough to break through the clutter and get a prospect's attention at little or no cost. Remember that nobody notices normal, so sometimes you have to break the rules to get through to that prospect and build a relationship with them.

If you have face to face contact and run a small to mid-sized business, then this is a great idea for reaching out to your prospect list. On a hot afternoon, load up a cooler full of Popsicles, ice cream bars, or cold lemonade, and go customer to customer serving everybody a treat on a hot afternoon. I doubt anyone has done it for them in the past and it's unlikely anyone other than you will do it again in the future. It's a great opportunity to hand someone something free and refreshing to remind them that you truly want their business.

Assignment

Get your group together and brainstorm some things you could do, such as the popsicle and ice cream idea. There are many opportunities with holidays and special events. Be creative and reach out to prospects. Don't just wait for them to come to you.

Epilogue

Most people are looking for something different. They don't know what they want, but they'll know it when they see it. Make sure they see you!

43

Go In Naked

We've repeatedly pointed out that making cold calls and developing new customers is not for the faint of heart. Cold calling requires a tough hide, a strong spirit, and a persistence very few people have. That's why the failure rate in selling is so incredibly high. One of the key strategies for achieving success is to not look like a salesperson out to shove merchandise down a prospect's throat.

Sandy was an attractive, enthusiastic, and sincere sales rep when she hit the road for the very first week. On Friday, she reported back to her sales manager that her sales productivity that week had been $00.00. He was baffled why she had no success, because even a dog with an order form tied around his tail should occasionally get somebody to take it off and fill it out. By making sales calls with her the next week, he identified her problem. She would go into an unknown prospect armed with two briefcases full of literature that screamed, "Here comes a salesperson! Here comes a salesperson!" and they would duck or avoid her like a rabbit getting out of the way of a shotgun. She had to learn to go in naked on those early calls and learn about the prospect long before she ever tried to sell them.

> ### *Assignment*
>
> Learn to go in naked and to ask questions. That's the only way you're going to find the needs, problems, and opportunities of your prospects. This information will help you go back later and make that presentation with your two briefcases of information.

Epilogue

Most people are looking for something that separates your product or service from all the others. Find that creative approach, and dare to be different.

44

Believe It or Not

Believe it or not, prospects and customers will stretch the truth, especially when they tell you their side of an incident, mistake, or problem they had while trying to do business with you. Before you go on a rampage accusing your staff of stupidity or mismanagement in handling the customer, be sure and get their side of the story first.

Assignment

Think like a judge and give everyone a chance to be heard before arriving at a decision. Often you will find that the customer is wrong.

When Harry went to the warehouse looking for Debbie, who had filled an order incorrectly for a customer that morning, he was smoking mad. They had tried and tried to get this customer's business for a long time and now, just when they closed the deal, Debbie screwed it all up.

But Harry listened to Debbie's side of the story before he went ballistic. Not only did Debbie believe she had filled the customer's order just as he wanted it, she still had his notes to back her up. Sure enough, Debbie was right and the customer was trying to save his ego and blame Debbie. Harry learned to get all sides of the story before making a judgment. Harry complimented Debbie and told the office to close the prospect's line of credit. He didn't want a new customer who had already proven he would lie to cover himself. That day Debbie grew a foot taller because of her boss' trust in her!

Epilogue

When your employees are right, stand by them, even if it upsets a prospect or customer. Your associates will respect you for it. After all, right is right!

45

Try Something Different

E-mail is a great communication tool if you can get your prospects to respond to you. Getting them to answer your e-mails may take creativity and humor. Often people don't respond because they are busy on work overload, or simply don't know what to say to you. Try something different to catch their attention and get them to e-mail you back.

One sales rep experimented with different kinds of e-mails and found something that worked frequently for prospects who had been failing to respond to him. He would write something like this:

Assignment

Try getting creative about e-mailing some of your more reluctant prospects. But make certain you target only prospects who will respond favorably to this kind of humor.

Dear Mr. Jones,

I've stopped by several times to see you and tried to get you on the phone to share an exciting proposal. Since I've not heard from you, I thought maybe one of the following things had happened: (1) You've been dragged into the outback by wild dingoes and are being held hostage. (2) You won the lottery, and now have millions and millions, and you no longer need to talk to me. (3) Wild women have discovered you are single, and you have had to go into hiding to escape the mobs that are after your body.

If you get a chance, or you come back from one of these three situations, please e-mail me back. Let's plan to get together to share how we can help you make some extra money.

Thanks!

Epilogue
If you do what everybody else does, then you'll get the same results that everybody else gets, which is generally pitiful. Try something different.

46

Customize, Customize, Customize

In a recent restaurant survey, 74 percent of people questioned said the number one thing they like to have in a restaurant is a salad bar. Why? Because they can make the salad their own way. They can have a little of this, a lot of that, and some of the other. They can make the salad exactly as they like it, with the right mix of ingredients, dressing, and croutons just for them. In today's world, people want a product that is truly customized, and is as individual as their personal taste.

> **Assignment**
>
> Think about how you can customize your products and services to fit your prospect's needs. People don't want one size fits all.

When Sue confronted her boss as a new employee, she asked him, "Do you know what's standard around here?" Her boss said "No, what is it?" And her answer was, "Nothing. Every customer wants something different. They want it their way." Her boss looked at her and said "You're right. Why don't we do it that way?" Think about what clothing stores do when you buy a nice suit. The first thing they do is tailor it to fit you. They shorten the sleeves, move the buttons, take a little out of the coat, and hem the pants or skirt. Suddenly you've got the product you want, detailed just the way you like.

> **Epilogue**
>
> *The more you can fit your products and services to the needs and wants of your customers, the more likely you are to win prospects over to become long-term customers.*

47

Little Things with Big Payoffs

Oftentimes potential customers comment on little things, the end result of which can be huge payoffs if you listen, change, and react to their feedback. Listening, and demonstrating that those changes are important, sends a huge message about how much you care.

A local library had just completed a multimillion dollar renovation and addition. It was beautiful and well-done. There was even a button to push that would automatically open the door for people with special needs. However, as a gentleman in a wheelchair approached the door, it became obvious that the doorway was too narrow and his power wheelchair barely slipped through. They needed to put an automatic opener on the second part of the door so that both doors would open to accommodate those visitors in wheelchairs. The gentleman made his way to the desk to explain the problem to the librarian, but she had all the empathy and sympathy of a drill sergeant. Her body language, her facial expression, and her reaction

> **Assignment**
>
> Make it a rule that everyone within your organization or company write down any feedback that could be considered important by management.

to his comments sent the message that she could not have cared less. Do you care about the little things that bring big results from your potential customers? Listening to them and making even minor changes and adjustments can send a huge message about your willingness to accommodate their needs.

Epilogue

Showing empathy and sympathy is the best way to convince customers that you are serious about meeting their needs.

48

Being Different

Joel Weldon has often said "Figure out what everybody else is doing, and don't do it." To be recognized in the clutter of today's market, you've got to figure out a better way, a different way, and a more affordable way, to keep telling your story. One of the ways to do that is to look at the changes going on in the marketplace.

With the popularity of the internet and e-mail, there have been some dramatic changes in the ways people communicate. Some of the things left behind that can pay off for you are your fax machine, letters, postcards, and the good old telephone. Those things today get attention because people have almost stopped using them. Consider how you can revise the fax, the postcard, the letter, and especially the phone call to keep in touch with prospects and customers. Analyze what your competition is doing, and don't do it.

Assignment

Study your competition and the marketplace, then devise new and innovative approaches that your competitors are not using. Try going back to snail mail to be different.

Find a different and better way to break through the clutter. The opportunities are everywhere.

> **Epilogue**
> *If you always do what you've always done, you'll always get what you've always gotten. You have to make changes to win customers.*

49

Do What Others Don't

While some messages are ideal to be e-mailed or faxed, there are some things that should never be sent that way. It's all too easy to cop out on doing what should be done for a thank you, invitation, or confidential message. By simply sending an e-mail, you are also sending a message that it's not important enough or confidential enough for you to send it the more traditional way.

In most areas of the country, there are stores that feature paper goods and discount greeting cards. In fact, some of them are so affordable it is almost ridiculous. Our recommendation is that you stock up on thank-you cards, invitations, birthday cards, and blank cards with no message inside. Get in the habit of recognizing people, inviting them to special events, thanking them for what they do, and also celebrating

> **Assignment**
> When you have the materials on hand, from cards to stamps to addresses, it's easy to do something that other's don't. You've got to systemize these types of mailings or they won't get done.

things like birthdays or anniversaries. By using traditional mailing methods, you'll be different, because most people are simply sending an e-mail. Prospects will recognize your extra effort, and they will reward you for it. Remember, you're building a relationship. You should do personal things for people with whom you have a relationship!

Epilogue

First we make our habits, then our habits make us. Get in the habit of using the more traditional ways to communicate that other people have abandoned, and you will stand out in the crowd.

50

Learn From Chameleons

We want to do business with people who are most like us. That is where your appearance and behaviors can work for you, or against you. Learn from the chameleon, which can change the appearance of it's skin to match the color underneath or behind it. It can go from green to black to blue to suit its surroundings. How can you change to be more like your customer?

Nido is a highly success- ful banker, entrepreneur, and

Assignment

What does your customer wear for a casual lunch as opposed to a formal dinner? What do they wear for presentations or meetings or celebrations? Study your customer, and then become a chameleon.

---

professional speaker. His closet features outfits for every occasion, from meeting with a CEO to blending in with a group of technical people. You can bet he will look most like them. How does Nido do it? He studies what other people do. What do they wear? What shoes do they wear? He will even call ahead and talk to a client to get some feedback on appropriate apparel. There's nothing funnier than to see someone show up in a suit and tie when everyone else is in blue jeans, or to see someone show up in blue jeans when everyone else is in a suit and tie. Learn from Nido, and learn to look like your customer so they will want to do business with you.

Epilogue

Your appearance can work for or against you. The chameleon teaches us to blend in for success!

51

Beware of First Appearences

We all know that you never get a second chance to make a first impression. But there's another part to that rule that says *You never get a second chance to judge people if you judge them wrong in the first place.* If you judge a customer's ability to buy, or their willingness to become a long-term customer, based on their appearance, their dress code, or their body language, it's easy to make a huge mistake. You can't tell what's on the inside by what's on the outside, and you can't tell their net worth, their ability to spend money, or their ability to borrow money based on their appearance. The best way is to assume that every person could be a prospect who could buy, and then

> **Assignment**
>
> Learn not to make snap judgments based on appearance. Ask some key questions to qualify a prospect rather than just depending on their appearance.

sort them out as you ask questions and get to know them.

The owner of a small high-performance auto shop had been having a tough day when a young customer came in and began to ask prices and availability on a page-long list of high-performance items. Somehow the owner managed to keep a smile on his face as he quoted price after price. However, inside he was telling himself "This is a waste of time. This young person could never afford to buy this stuff." After pricing many thousands of dollars of merchandise, the young man looked at the shop owner and said "Okay, I'll take it." To which the owner responded, "You'll take what?" The customer said "Everything you just quoted." With that, he pulled out a roll of hundred dollar bills to pay for what was on hand and what had to be ordered. The owner learned a great lesson that day. Never judge a person by what's on the outside, and never assume a prospect can't or won't buy based on their appearance.

Epilogue

There's no way of knowing for sure whether the person with whom you're talking is a pauper or a millionaire. The best way is to let them qualify themselves rather than running the risk of judging them incorrectly.

52

Prospecting Requires Being a Super-Sleuth

You can never know too much about a prospect to whom you'd like to sell. The more you learn, the more likely you are to win over that potential account. There is no excuse to be uninformed in today's information-rich society, where you have resources like your local library and the Internet.

When a consultant was invited to meet with Flagstar Bank to consider doing promotional work for them, he downloaded every page from their Website and learned everything about them, from their mission statement to their philosophy of customer service, from their growth plans to their financial performance in recent years. When he walked in to meet with the Flagstar management, he was armed and ready to discuss where they'd been, and where they were going.

Assignment

Think of yourself as a detective building a case. You must convince a prospect to become a customer, so be sure to do your research first!

Epilogue
Knowledge is power. If you don't know enough about a prospect, the only reason is because you haven't tried hard enough.

53

Inspired Employees
Lead to Dedicated Customers

If you haven't purchased and read the book, *151 Quick Ideas for Inspiring Your Staff*, I encourage you to run out and buy a copy right now. Not because we want to make a sale, but because it will help you in growing a group of excited people who are ready, willing, and able to make your company a success. Can you think of anything more important? The real secret to inspiring people is to get them involved and give them a reputation to live up to. Show them that you have high expectations of them, and then watch them follow through and prove you right.

> **Assignment**
>
> Analyze each of your people and decide what unique gifts they have and what things they do well.

Jerry, the owner of a mid-sized company, hired a comptroller named Mae. He soon began calling her his human computer. She was indeed a genius at organizing and running their office, and he enjoyed working with her so much he bragged about her to everyone who would listen. Frequently, Jerry would give tours of his business to prospective customers, and he would always make a point to take them to Mae's office and introduce her. She became a partner in helping grow the business and took great pride in her work. Give your people a great reputation to live up to, and then get out of their way and let them do it. It's a successful formula that will not fail you.

Epilogue
People become what they see of themselves in their mind's eye. When you lift them up and put them on a pedestal, they will perform to that level.

54

The C-Y-A Factor

More than one sales rep knows the agony of defeat. Sometimes defeat comes from failing to get permission before taking an action, which can result in anything from a small dose of criticism to a big dose of being fired. Adopt the rule of *When in Doubt, Check it Out*. Get permission before you proceed on anything that might backfire on you later!

An advertising agency recently placed an ad for Wal-Mart on the west coast without running it by Wal-Mart Management first. It was very out of style with what Wal-Mart would typically do, and customers and prospects alike were insulted. Ultimately the agency was fired and lost a very lucrative account. If

> **Assignment**
> Make it a rule that if your gut reaction gives you any concern, you will make time to check it out. You may even want the customer to initial or sign off on what you're about to do so you can C-Y-A (Cover Your...)

they had gotten that ad cleared with Wal-Mart management, even on a local level, they probably would still have that account. Unfortunately, they're now out doing a great deal of prospecting for new customers. But they've learned an important lesson, to always check with the appropriate authorities before making any big decisions.

Epilogue

Sometimes it's easier to get forgiveness than get permission, but to be safe, always use the rule of "When in doubt, check it out."

55

The Best Prospect Ever

Prospecting for new customers can be expensive, hard work, and eat up your time like a hungry goat in your neighbor's yard. The best prospect has always been, still is, and will always be the one who contacts you. You are starting with a potential customer who knows they have a need or want, is ready to buy, and is giving you a vote of confidence by reaching out to you first.

Assignment

As long as it's legal and ethical, we can call, poke, push, pull, incentivize, motivate, stimulate, remind, inspire, and do anything we can to get prospects to call us.

Renee, a response and marketing consultant from Florida, believes that there are three important prospecting principles to remember at all costs: (1) Your success will be determined by the quality and quantity of your prospect list; (2) Your prospect must hear from you a minimum of every 30 days to maintain top-of-mind awareness; and (3) Getting prospects to call you means making them multiple offers.

Epilogue

When customers call you, they see themselves as a welcome guest, but when you attempt to sell them, they see you as a necessary pest.

56

Connect Like Velcro

Every person has common needs, such as the need to be wanted, needed, and accepted. When you make emotional connections with your prospects and get to know them as a person, you will go a long way to establishing rapport with them. It is easy to forget that prospects have a life beyond the office. If you can make an emotional connection with your prospect, you should connect to them like Velcro and never lose it!

When Steve attended a family reunion, he was amazed at how quickly the years seemed to disappear as he talked with his long-lost relatives. That was because they had a common

> ### Assignment
> Write yourself a note that people buy from people, and learn to do inner-views and listen carefully.

discussion about the family, and it was easy to pick up where they had left off years before. Your prospects are ready, willing, and waiting to establish a relationship with you if you can do an inner-view with them. That means getting to know what's inside of them, like where they were born, where they went to school, their hobbies, their families, their pets, and their greatest accomplishments. Learn to establish at least one thing with each prospect that you can continue as a dialogue each time you connect with them. Find common ground and they will become not only your customer, but also your friend.

Epilogue

You can make more friends in two weeks getting interested in them than you can in two years trying to get them interested in you.

57

Whatever It Takes

Good prospectors maximize their time and multiply their efforts by using affordable resources to call on their customers. One such way is to use your friendly U.S. Postal Service carrier in those well-known blue uniforms. Think about how you can use priority mail, which is affordable, available, and cost-effective, to send a special message to your prospects. Priority mail gets attention, and it says what's inside the package is very important. Prospects pay attention to it because it is different from the pile of regular mail, which is probably just bills and advertisements.

Develop a philosophy of using W-I-T to gain and retain prospects and customers. W-I-T stands for Whatever It Takes. One of the best things you can do that can have a huge impact on your success is to keep top-of-mind-awareness with your prospects, especially your top 10 list, by sending them a priority mail package once in a while. They'll be impressed, and they will know you are serious about wanting their business. It's a great investment, because it works. So do "Whatever It Takes" to maximize your prospecting efforts and win new customers.

Assignment

Go to your local post office and get a stack of priority envelopes, mailers, boxes, and labels. Determine the postage, remembering that you can access postage over the internet, so you can handle all this from your office. Then routinely communicate with your prospects using Whatever It Takes.

Epilogue

You can multiply your impact on prospects by using priority mail and the thousands of hardworking postal carriers across the country.

58

Love Those Freebies

If you are like most people trying to gain new customers, it is likely you will serve a diversity of businesses and occupations. For example, your prospective customers may include the butcher, the baker, the candlestick maker, and many more. One of the best ways to learn more about your prospect's interest is from their trade and professional journals. Every industry and every trade has specialty magazines and trade journals that contain a treasury of tips, tricks, trends, and other information you need to know to be able to talk to your prospective customers.

When new employees come to work for Rodney, the very first thing he does is get the reply cards out of the various trade journals, and have his new employees sign up to for the mailing list. Most trade journals are absolutely free and are supported by industry advertising. He encourages his employees to make time each month to go through these journals and keep up with the various industries. His office currently gets about a dozen different trade journals, and they are all well-used. Nothing flatters a prospective customer more than to know that you have taken the time to learn more about what they do, what their interests are, and what challenges they face.

> ### Assignment
> Visit the kinds of businesses you're interested in learning more about. Most of them get some kind of trade journal and will be glad to share their reply cards.

Epilogue
If you want to know more the intricacies of any business or profession, there's no better way to learn than from these free professional journals.

59

Do You Qualify?

One hard and fast rule in sports, and in competing for customers, is that you can never win if you're always playing defense. Consider turning the selling process on its head and approaching customers to see if they qualify to do business with you. By screening customers to see if they qualify, you can create one of the great motivational principles, to build an eager want within a prospective customer base.

One financial planner has developed a track record of helping his clients earn a great return on their money. The number of referrals sent to him is something most salespeople can only fantasize about.

> ### *Assignment*
> To make this principle work, you've got to be able to stack up the benefits of what you're offering.

He's in the enviable position of being able to tell prospects that his services are not for everyone, and that they need to meet to see if they are a good fit. He is actually interviewing prospects to see if he will allow them to come aboard as customers. By the time the interview is over, most prospects are begging him to take on their investments. Can you turn the selling process on its head and qualify your customers?

Epilogue
It seems that the more exclusive an item is, the more people want that item. Make your prospects want to be your customers, and develop an exclusive client list.

60

Before You Open Up

If your business attracts customers at specific opening times, like my favorite coffee shop hangout that opens at six a.m., then nothing sends a stronger negative message than walking in the door and watching the employees scramble to get their act together. The coffee's not made, there's no money in the register, and several employees are late. That's a poor way to start the day.

> ### Assignment
> Make it a point to be open and ready when you are supposed to be. That's just meeting customer expectations. Then go on to delight them with your products and services.

Consider investing in having one or more employees come in early to get everything ready so that when you open the door, you're ready to serve customers. They should be able to depend on you to serve their needs and offer them the products they want, all with delightful customer service.

It's the professional way to run a business, and the small investment in additional payroll will definitely pay off.

> ### Epilogue
> *Being prepared gives your staff the confidence to smile at customers. It also lets them know that you're prepared and ready to serve or help them.*

61

Tell and Sell

I'm a confessed nut about prospecting at little or no cost. One important step is to have your name and contact information on everything you print, sell, make, take, or give away that could direct a prospect back to you. The best strategy is to have your Website visible on everything from pens to notepads, and calendars to tape measures. If you leave these items with prospects, either purposely or accidentally, the prospect will eventually notice your contact information and either call you, or check out your Website.

One prospect couldn't remember our name and phone number, and had unfortunately lost our business card. But luckily, he found a pen that I had left there several years ago, and it had our Website on it. He was able to visit our Website, and reach us through our contact information. Since then, he has become a huge customer,

Assignment

Teach your staff that nothing is to leave your business without having your contact information on it. It could be a Website, e-mail address, or phone number. Just make certain they have a way to reach you!

and is likely to spend many dollars in the future. We would never have gotten their account had we not taken the step of being visible and giving people a way to contact us. You have to remember to tell and sell to meet prospects and make customers.

Epilogue
A funny thing happens when you don't promote yourself. Nothing!

62

Make Sure Prospects Can Find You

One great and easily affordable way to reach prospects is by using e-mail. Not only is this a convenient way for customers to reach you, but it can also give you the opportunity to respond in a well-thought-out method. E-mail can be done on your own terms and your own schedule, without forcing you to be quick on your feet. You can take the time to gather price quotes, efficiency statistics, or other data that might come in handy when speaking with a prospect.

Unfortunately, about 20 percent or more of all the contact links on Websites are broken, so when you click on the name or e-mail address, it either doesn't connect or gets bounced back. Some businesses confuse, and indirectly sabotage, the ability of prospects to find them by frequently changing their e-mail addresses. When dropping established e-mail addresses, you close the door on a prospect, which could make you lose the sale of the century! Don't let this happen to you.

> ### Assignment
>
> When discontinuing the use of an e-mail address, consider keeping it up and checking it daily and simply providing a link to your current address until you are absolutely confident that no one will attempt to contact your through the old address. Another method is to retain the domain name and have the ISP redirect e-mail to your new Website or e-mail address.

Epilogue

Out of sight means out of mind. Make sure that prospects can find you whenever they need to.

63

Leave Your Prospects a Trail to Follow

You've heard the old adage about leaving a trail of bread crumbs to lead you back home when you go out exploring. That's what you should be trying to do with prospects. Leave a trail that reminds them of your company and that you want their business. This can be anything with your name and logo on it, from an ink pens to a baseball caps, from memo pads to golf balls. The long-term goal is to give reminders and create an outpost in your prospect's mind. If you leave bread crumbs for them, they will eventually find their way back to you.

A busy association executive had entertained a prospective insurance pro-

Assignment

Find a source for logo and identity items. Buy up a variety of items and get them out on the highways and byways where your prospects operate.

vider numerous times. He failed to notice that each time this insurance agent called on him, he also left him a small gift. One day he looked at the top of his desk, and he had a memo holder, a leather address book, a large desktop calendar, an ink pen holder, ink pens, rulers, and more, all with the insurance company's name, logo, and phone number. When his current association insurance program hit a speed bump and they had to source another vendor, it was easy to decide who to call. Their name and phone number was everywhere. Not a bad investment for some logo identity items that were left behind.

Epilogue

In today's over-communicated world, where it is nearly impossible to get your advertising message out to customers, this concept is a winner that you can do with little or no hassle.

64

Learn from the F.B.I.

The Federal Bureau of Investigation, better known as the F.B.I., is known coast to coast for their 10 Most Wanted list. Each week they review and update the list, removing those people who've been captured, or adding people who warrant it. You can use the same idea to focus your time, energy, and resources on your best prospects by having your own Top 10 Most Wanted list.

Terry, a very effective sales manager, believed that if his salespeople were

Assignment

Make a Top 10 wanted list, and develop the weekly discipline to update it. Be sure to make assignments so that your staff knows who is responsible for each item on the list.

trying to sell to just any old prospect, they would probably do a poor job and not sell anything. He learned he had to get them focused on their best sales opportunities. Each Monday morning, he required his salespeople to complete a new Top 10 list for action that week. He also required them to write alongside each of those 10 the action or activities they were going to take that week to try to turn that prospect into a customer. By having them focused, and having a copy of their Top 10 action plan, it kept them on target to go after their best prospects.

Epilogue

Confucius once said "A man who chases two rabbits catches none." Be focused and know exactly what you are trying to catch.

65

Keeping Top-of-Mind-Awareness

What do other people think of you? At age 20, you worry about what everybody's thinking of you. At age 40, you don't care what people are thinking about you. And when you get to age 60, you find out they weren't thinking of you in the first place.

The goal with all your prospects is to keep T-O-M-A, which means Top-of-Mind-Awareness. One sign in a store said "We wouldn't worry about what people think of us if we realized how seldom they do." Keeping top-of-mind-awareness is an awesome task, but it can be accomplished. For example, on

> **Assignment**
>
> Take every opportunity to maintain T-O-M-A with your customers and prospects. Try something at least once a month. And don't ever forget them while you are on vacation.

your next vacation, take along a set of labels or the addresses of your best prospects. While you're sunbathing on the beach or sitting beside the pool, send some "I wish you were here" type postcards back to your prospects. Every tourist area has them available. They are affordable, and they're a fun way to communicate and keep T-O-M-A with your prospects.

Epilogue

You need to be creative different to consistently maintain Top-of-Mind-Awareness with your prospects and customers.

66

The Proof of the Pudding

The proof of the pudding is not in the tasting, but in whether people return for a second helping. You can get anyone to try a bite of your favorite recipe, but if they don't care for it, getting them to take that second bite is going to be tough. The same is true with prospecting for customers. Getting new customers is simply a function of your willingness to spend on promotion and advertising, and to do cost-cutting and giveaways to bring them in the door. If you do all that, you can get the new customers.

The question however, is whether you can get them back again.

While visiting a new church in our area, I was interested to notice that although this beautiful facility had been there for many years, there weren't enough parishioners for the Sunday

> **Assignment**
>
> Develop a system to track repeat business and customer longevity. This will help you identify why customers leave, and why they come back.

morning service to fill more than a few rows. Something was wrong. At the end of the service, the pastor asked us to sign their visitor logbook. The book was filled ten inches thick, and had hundreds of pages logging where visitors had signed in, went out the door, and never came back. The problem with this church was not that they weren't getting prospects; it was that they weren't converting them to customers. Keep your focus, not just on the first sale, but on the second and all future sales. If you don't get repeat business, you're never going to be successful as a prospector, because repeat business is the proof of the pudding.

Epilogue

Your goal is to have customers for life. Build your system to support that mission.

67

What About Tomorrow?

The best way to ensure that a customer will return to your company in the future is to make sure that your associates understand the importance of delightful customer service, because it's the only way to guarantee that the customer will return.

The owner of a quick lube/oil change center found a masterful way to convince his employees about the importance of customer service. He asked each person to ask one simple question when serving a customer: "Is what I'm doing today going to bring this customer back tomorrow?"

> ### Assignment
> Get your group to brainstorm what it will take to get the customer back the next time. Reinforce the idea that the next sale is just as important as the current one, and they will be sure to treat each customer with respect.

They had the sale for today. The issue was to get them to come back in the future. This savvy business owner realized that fixing cars was only part of their job.

> ### Epilogue
> *Always remember that when you fix a problem, you have to remember to fix the customer.*

68

Your Elevator Speech

There's an old saying that you never get a second chance to make a good first impression. When someone asks who you are and what you do, how do you respond? You need to know your elevator speech in sixty seconds or less to be able to tell them who you are, what you sell or what you serve, and why a customer should do business with you. You may only get one chance to make that good first impression.

A business owner was interested in changing his local zoning laws. When he met a member of his local legislature, they got on the elevator together to go up to the conference room. The legislator pushed the button

> ### *Assignment*
> Script your elevator speech, and make sure everybody in your company can recite it word for word so they're all on the same page.

for the 12th floor, and when the elevator door closed, he turned around and said "What do you want from me and what can you do for me? Tell me in 60 seconds or less." Amazingly, this business owner was prepared. He had a well-defined answer, and by the time the elevator stopped on the 12th floor, the legislator was ready to help him, and also to get the benefit of having the business owner as a promoter for the upcoming reelection campaign. Can you tell people in 60 seconds or less why they should buy from you?

Epilogue
When someone slams the door, don't put your foot in it. Stick your head in it so you can keep talking.

69

Point Out the Problem

If you've watched a television infomercial, then you know how problems can be exaggerated and made bigger than they really are. In fact, most infomercials are for products that solve problems that most people don't even recognize!

Have you ever heard of halitosis? Although the condition of bad breath has been around for ages, the word to describe it was not well known until the early part of the 20th century. The term halitosis was made popular by a salesman who had invented mouthwash. He found a problem, advertised and exaggerated it, and then sold the solution and made himself a fortune. When you find a problem, be sure to point it out to your prospects. Your solution will be a breath of fresh air!

> ## *Assignment*
>
> Define the problem, and then work to find ways to make the problem common knowledge. Once your prospects know that the problem exists, they will be eager for your solutions.

Epilogue
People don't buy solutions to problems that they don't know they have.

70

Go After Lost Customers

Sometimes the best customer to get is the one you had in the past, the one who defected and went to the competition. They may find that they aren't as happy as they thought they'd be. Your continued efforts to win them back could result in regaining a good customer, perhaps an even better customer, than you had before. Oftentimes lost customers are simply waiting for you to invite them back.

The owner of a dental laboratory lost one of their big customers who represented more than 40 percent of their regular business. Although he tried, the customer failed to return the owner's phone calls. After much debate, he decided to try something a little different. He bought a sympathy card and wrote a personal note to the business owner. He explained he wasn't sure what had happened and why they were unhappy, but it was a shame that they weren't doing business together anymore, because he believed they were good for each other. He was offering his sympathy that they would have to do business somewhere else. He sent the card to the business owner, and soon got a phone call. The customer wanted to sit down and talk, and soon returned as a loyal customer. Don't give up on lost customers.

> ### *Assignment*
> Keep a lost customer list, and keep track of your efforts to win them back.

> ### Epilogue
> *You know what a lost customer can be, and how your relationship can improve if you make the effort.*

71

Free Still Works

Of the most powerful words you can use in selling your marketing message, the word *free* is still at the top of the list. In fact, one marketing magazine noted in a recent article that free food and drink still brings out more people than a great guest speaker or a high-impact seminar topic. We all love to get something for nothing.

> **Assignment**
>
> Always pre-inspect the place where you plan to take them for a meal, and make arrangements for the quiet corner or that table where you won't be interrupted too much. It's worth the planning.

If you have a high-value potential customer that you've not been able to win over, consider offering them a free gourmet meal, and see what happens. There are some key words to communicate within your invitation that can be a big help in getting them to take advantage of your free offer. First, make sure they understand that they are under no obligation to join you for that free meal. Second, they will be your guest and that you are going to pay. Third, there will be no high pressure sales pitch while they are dining. Keeping them safe will encourage them to say yes to your free offer.

Epilogue

Although many claim that there's no such thing as a free lunch, you can prove them wrong. Offer a low-pressure event with lots of free gifts or food, and watch the customers come out of the woodwork!

72

Out of Sight Means Out of Mind

If it often feels like we spend our lives standing in line, you're right! Of the average 70 year life span, five years are spent waiting to be waited upon. No one likes to wait in line when it's not necessary, and no one likes to see employees in your place of business do things that aren't related to direct customer service. Although sometimes these other tasks are necessary to the business, you should try and get that work done out of sight of the customer. The people standing in line won't become upset if they see every associate working busily to serve their needs.

The fast food industry has gotten a black eye in recent years, and their customer service rating has slipped in each annual survey, because you'll often see twenty people working behind the counter, cooking, scrubbing, or cleaning, and only one person waiting on customers. If you have situations where people need to work on things other than serving customers, get them out of the customer's sight so they'll be out of mind.

Assignment

Teach everyone that they need to stay out of the customer's visibility when they are not directly serving the customer. Perhaps more importantly, empower them to decide that customers are more important that what they are doing, and get them to help out with customer service. Customers just don't understand why they cannot be waited on.

> **Epilogue**
>
> *Customers don't want to be served very soon; they want to be served now. The business that can eliminate waiting in line will be the one that wins the new customers.*

73

E-mail: Friend or Foe?

Electronic mail has become the most prominent method of communication in our modern society. Even the post office is feeling the effect of e-mail. The volume of letters has dropped significantly, while the population and the number of businesses continue to increase. E-mail can be a great tool for prospecting, or it can be your worst enemy.

One corporate person recently shared that she gets over 200 e-mails a day, and it is about all she can do to keep up with them. What's even worse is that she estimates 70 to 80 percent of them are unnecessary. That means that you have to be careful about using e-mail. First, you must make sure the subject line is personal to the person to whom it's going. Many e-mails are simply deleted without being opened, because they scream SPAM. Second, never

Assignment

Collect every e-mail address of every prospect, and create an e-mail series so powerful, they will look forward to it every week or month.

send broadcast e-mails without getting the permission of the people you put on your list. Third, when you've got something of benefit to the receiver, don't be afraid to send it by e-mail, but make your message short and sweet. Lastly, if in doubt, check it out. Get permission before you send an e-mail.

Epilogue

When used correctly, e-mail can be your greatest prospecting tool. But used without caution, it can become your worst nightmare.

74

Keep the Lights On

It's unlikely your business can justify offering 24-hours a day and seven-days a week service, and it's possible your customers don't need or want that level of help. But today there are simple and affordable ways to show your customers they aren't stuck when your door is closed and the lights are out.

Arriving at a major chain drugstore location, one customer was exasperated to find them closed. Then on the door, she noticed a sign directing her to the nearest 24-hour pharmacy. She was thrilled. What can you do during non-business hours to help your customers? Would an emergency phone answering service be of value? Would customers benefit from having a cell phone number or beeper to call in an emergency? Would a 24-hour help line answer their questions and hold them off until you open? And what can you do when the phone rings after hours? Rather than let them just hear it ring, you could get an answering machine, and tell them when you can serve them.

> **Assignment**
>
> Find out what your competitors are doing in your industry, and then do more than they are. Look at what people are doing outside your business, and adopt and adapt their ideas and strategies.

You can always offer a variety of options, from your Webpage to your telephone to your emergency services, to let your customers know that when the lights are out, you want them to come back when the lights are on.

Epilogue

We are no longer an 8-to-5, Monday-to-Friday country of workers. People have diverse schedules, and they're looking for services when many traditional businesses have turned out the lights and gone home. The people who can accommodate them will win and retain their business.

75

One Magic Word

When you deal with customers, the magic word is not *if*, but *when*. You are eventually going to encounter a prospect or a new customer who is unhappy with you, your products, services, or your company. Knowing how to deal with emotional issues can turn upset customers into loyal buyers and be the pivotal point of either losing their business or winning their hearts.

When a telephone service manager encountered a customer who was upset, he listened attentively and then asked the magic question: "What can I do to make you happy?" The customer first said that he believed he deserved a $400 credit against his bill for the time their phone service was down. The manager quickly agreed and said "Will that make you happy?" The fellow then said

that he wanted to get some service people out to his home and have his phones fixed by four o'clock. The manager said "My very best people are already en route. Will you be happy if your phones are up and running by 4:00 p.m.?" The customer said he wanted one more thing, an apology. With that, the telephone executive apologized for the errors they had made in serving him. He knew that the secret formula to dealing with upset people is to ask the question, "What will make you happy?" and then whenever possible, settle the dispute on their terms.

Epilogue

Why does the happy concept work? Because you're negotiating happiness on the customer's terms, and when you agree to what they want, they feel empowered.

76

Quality Speaks Volumes

For a number of years a woman did a television commercial for Hanes Underwear. Her slogan was, "It doesn't say

Hanes until I say it says Hanes" and it was a huge success in selling their undergarments. For many years quality control in America deteriorated so drastically that overseas competitors stole a large portion of the market share. Today however, we're back and doing better than ever. But the painful lessons we learned about building a reputation for quality products and services has been expensive.

> **Assignment**
>
> Quality is the cumulative effect of many choices. Make a decision today that you're going to drive your company with superior quality. Then communicate that goal to customers and prospects.

The late W. Edwards Deming was respected worldwide as a proponent of quality. He said that quality didn't really cost, but was in fact a profit center. Quality products result in fewer rejects, less maintenance, less down-time, extended performance, more enjoyment of usage, and an increase in customer loyalty.

Epilogue

There always will be a top-end buyer who's willing to pay a premium price for quality products and services.

77

Keeping up With Technology

We live in an ever-changing world. By the time you buy a new computer or a piece of equipment, it's already out of date because there's a better one coming down the assembly line. The challenge is to keep up, have the latest in technology and equipment, and maintain your position in the marketplace. The secret is to budget a fixed amount that will allow you to keep up and remain a state-of-the-art operation. Staying on the cutting edge will give you an advantage when turning prospects into customers!

There's a printing shop in Las Vegas that has a policy of investigating any and every piece of new equipment that comes on the market. If they have a printing press that is only a year old and a new and better one is offered by the manufacturer, they investigate it to see if it's truly a better product. If it is, they immediately sell the one they have and buy the new that offers them the latest and greatest in features and benefits. Because they have the best in equipment and people, they also attract the best customers. Most of their printing is for Fortune 500 companies' annual reports and for the Las Vegas gambling casinos who want nothing but the best.

> ### *Assignment*
>
> Technology = productivity = competitiveness = great prospecting. Set up a review process for evaluating your technology against current standards. And don't forget to budget for upgrades!

> ### Epilogue
> *The world is moving on whether you do or not. The secret is to keep up with the latest technology to best serve your customers.*

78

Is Your Image Working for You?

Look around your company today, including the buildings, vehicles, offices, signage, and your trucks on the road. What kind of message are you sending to your prospects? How would you rate yourself as you look today? Would you say it's sad and definitely needs improvement? Would you say it's average or typical when compared to your competition? Or would you rate yourself as outstanding? It's important to take the time and analyze what your image is, and whether it's working for or against your long-term goals.

Mike's Car Wash is a highly successful regional group of car wash facilities. The appearance of their facilities is not typical or average, but it is definitely working for them. It begins with their huge colorful signage, their manicured lawns, their beautiful flowers, and their spotlessly clean and meticulously well-kept facilities. When you swing your car around to start through the conveyor belt, your car is given an extra treatment on the front and rear to steam clean those bugs and tar away. You are even greeted by two smiling Mike's employees in nothing less than shirt and tie. Can this really be a car wash?

> ### Assignment
>
> Take inventory of your company's image and set a goal that you will no longer accept the average. While being average may not work against you, being above average or outstanding will work for you. You will stand out in the crowd like a rose amongst the thorns.

Epilogue

Make sure your image is working for you. Because if it isn't, it's working against you. Why start the day by swimming uphill?

79

Don't Take It for Granted

One huge problem in getting new customers is falling into the trap of complacency. If you go in unprepared, and the competition follows you with a great dog and pony show, guess who gets the sale? You will be left asking what went wrong, and the competition will walk away with the customer.

A Las Vegas sales rep had an opportunity to make a presentation to a large organization. Because they knew him and he knew them, he debated what kind of sales presentation to make. Finally, he called one

> **Assignment**
>
> Ask yourself, am I too complacent? What do I really need to do to sell this prospect?

of his mentors who sat on that organization's board and asked what kind of presentation he recommended. The wise man said, "If you had never met this group, what kind of presentation would you make?" The sales rep responded that he would have a full-blown PowerPoint presentation, a custom book with all the details, and a room set up to sell the project. That is exactly what he did, and he had a very successful presentation. Always prepare as if you had never met your customer or prospect, even if you've done business with them before, and you'll be successful every time.

Epilogue

You will never fail by over-preparing. You'll only fail if you take your customers, or your success, for granted.

80

Beware of a Prescription Without a Diagnosis

Imagine seeing a new doctor, and without saying a word to you, she began to write out new prescriptions for you. She was doing so without getting your medical history, checking your vital signs, or even asking why you were there. Would you pay her for that visit or take those medications? It's very doubtful that you would feel comfortable doing so. Getting a prescription without a diagnosis is called malpractice!

When a plumbing wholesaler was desperately looking to increase sales and get new customers, he asked his will-call sales desk for suggestions to improve the business. They said the area needed to be spruced up, they needed a new counter, better uniforms, improved signage, and a nice place for their plumbing customers to come in and pick up their orders. The owner did exactly what his people recommended, but sales didn't go up at all. Why? Because it wasn't important to the customers! So he personally went out and made calls on his plumbing contractors and asked them what was critically important to them. They explained that having the right pieces was what they valued most. When he's missing just one gooseneck for a sink, the plumber is shut down and can't finish the job. Filling the order was what they valued most. He decided to guarantee every contractor that an order would be filled 100 percent complete within 24

> ### Assignment
>
> Always remember that a prescription without a diagnosis is called malpractice. What is really important to your customer, and how do you find out? Just ask!

hours. The program was a huge success, and his sales volume skyrocketed. Why? Because he prescribed what his customers needed.

Epilogue

What do your customers want from you? Find out what it is and give it to them.

81

Make It Easy to Buy

In recent years Americans have started paying more bills with credit and debit cards, than they do with cash or checks. It's a turning point that signals to businesses everywhere that they should be flexible with their accepted methods of payment.

There's a sign in a Las Vegas casino that says, "How would you like to pay? We accept gold dust, gold bars, Mastercard, Visa, American Express, Carte Blanche, Discover, and Diner's. We will take a company check, a personal check, or your traveler's check... Heck, we even take bad checks. And of course, we will take cash." Everybody has a good laugh when they see that sign, but they remember one thing. This casino

105

Assignment

Take inventory of how customers want to pay you. If you don't have the credit cards and check guarantee service, get them today! This will make it easy for customers to do business with you.

makes it easy to do business. How are you making it easy to conduct transactions, request service, or order inventory? Will you accept gold dust and gold bars? Do you take all the major credit cards? If you make it easy for the customer to buy from you, you'll convert prospects into customers faster than ever before.

Epilogue
We are a plastic society, and trying to fight it won't work. Make it easy for customers to do business. Don't create roadblocks and sabotage yourself.

82

Make Them Feel Safe

Dr. Carla Morgan has pointed out that virtually any potential customer you're going to talk to has been lied to, taken advantage of, and probably cheated at some point in their life. They have probably heard lots of promises that never came true. By addressing their need for safety and security, you have a high probability of winning over a prospect. Making them feel safe and secure when doing business with you is an important strategy in prospecting.

In convincing one of his most skeptical prospects, one sales rep found that the word "no" had a big payoff. As he communicated his desire to do business with them, he assured them again and again that there would be no risk because of his absolute, positive guarantee. There would be no selling, because all he wanted to do was point out how he could help. There would be no obligation, because they would have the right to say no with no hard feelings and no further pressure on his end, and no embarrassment.

> ### *Assignment*
> Get others to help you analyze where potential customers might feel risk, pressure, or obligation, and design a prospecting program that will overcome their objections.

He would never put them in a situation that would be awkward for them. And it worked, because he converted one of his most skeptical prospects. Make your customers feel safe. Take away the risk, manage the other issues, and watch what happens.

Epilogue
Admit it or not, Dr. Morgan says that fear is ever-present, and making people feel safe and secure is a very basic principle to get new customers.

83

Loose Lips Sink Prospects

It was during the Second World War that the phrase *loose lips sink ships* was used in propaganda posters to remind the American people not to divulge secrets. The same holds true in dealing with potential customers who are willing to share their confidences with you. Just make a promise to yourself that when prospects and customers share confidences with you, you will not divulge that information to anyone.

> ### *Assignment*
>
> Remember the rule that the only way two people can keep a secret is if one of them is dead, and don't ever share confidence.

When Bob called one of his key suppliers to discuss several internal problems he had, he opened the conversation by asking his supplier to keep totally quiet about some theft problems Bob had inside his business. Together, Bob and his supplier were able to formulate a plan to help Bob deal with the theft. More importantly, they cemented a relationship based on trust, which is the ultimate compliment anyone can give you. The supplier assured Bob that no one would be told about what was going on. He gave his word on that. Could a prospect or customer trust you in that same situation?

Epilogue

Say what you'll do and do what you say, and your predictability, trust, and honesty will pay off in a steady flow of new customers.

84

Building Trust

Trust is the most essential ingredient of all really great relationships, both personal and professional. Unfortunately, trust must be earned over time by consistent performance. It's very rare that a customer will trust you on the first day and with their first transaction.

Retailing giant Sam Walton recognized the value of trust as he built the Wal-Mart empire. He said, "If I could stand trust at the register, I would be home free. The reality is you must earn a customer's trust one customer, one transaction, and one day at a time." One thing you can do to gain more trust is to keep your promises and follow through, and then point it out to your prospect or customer. For example, you might say, "Bill, I told you I would have these for you today, and here they are." Or you might say, "Mary, I promised I would call you back on Wednesday, and today is Wednesday." When you do the right thing, make an issue of it, and wave your flag in the air. It will help you accelerate the process of building trust.

> **Assignment**
>
> Make a rule that a promise made is a promise kept. Remember that your word is your bond.

> **Epilogue**
> *Trust is more fragile than an egg, and you need to protect it every day, with every sale, and with every prospect or customer.*

85

Falling Out of the Dumb Tree

Do you believe you can build a successful long-term business that will attract new customers by lying, cheating, or deceiving customers? Do you believe your customers fell out of the dumb tree and hit every limb on the way down? That seems to be the way many businesses approach their customers, but they don't last long. Customers are not as dumb as many business people think they are. Abraham Lincoln once said "You can fool all of the people some of the time, and some of the people all of the time, but you cannot fool all of the people all of the time."

Assignment

Always tell the truth, the whole truth, and nothing but the truth. Build your reputation on that.

A business owner was finally able to buy a really high quality copier. He was excited about the many things it would do because they had a variety of needs in their office. One of their first projects was to run some postcard stock for a mailing they hoped to do that day. As they fed the postcard stock into the machine, it jammed and refused to print or copy anything. It was exasperating! When the copier service person arrived and they explained their problem, he looked at them and said "Our salesperson told you what? He told you this machine would run postcard stock? Sorry, but it won't!" How long do you think that salesman will succeed when he tells falsehoods?

> **Epilogue**
>
> *The single rule for honesty in winning customers is to say what you'll do and do what you'll say. Only by following this rule will you succeed at getting new customers.*

86

Consider Name-Dropping

We see everyone from sports greats to rock stars, and movie idols to political celebrities, attempting to sell us all sorts of items. The power of influence should never be overlooked in your attempt to win customers. There is real power when well-known people like celebrities or sports stars try to convince us that a specific product or service is good for us.

If you ask, many of your existing customers will give you a testimonial about how your products or services helped them. They might even allow you to use their photograph along with their quote. When Oprah features a book on her TV show, it is

> **Assignment**
>
> Ask yourself who on your customer roster could influence others to come aboard. Then ask for their help in developing testimonials.

guaranteed to sell a quarter of a million copies almost immediately, simply because she has so much credibility with the book-purchasing public. Think about how you could use testimonials, name-dropping, or perhaps a list of your existing customers to influence others to join you. But proceed with caution, and remember *When in Doubt, Check it Out*. Be sure to get your customer's permission to use their photograph, their name, or their testimonial.

Epilogue

If you're not convinced of the power of other people's influence, ask yourself why a book on Oprah's list sells millions of copies just because it has her stamp of approval.

87

Freebies Are Hard to Turn Down

Getting something free is hard to resist, and regardless of the prospect's loyalty to your competitor or their reluctance to consider you and your advantages, a freebie can often break through. Think about what you can do to get their patronage with offers that are almost unbelievable.

When a Phoenix manufacturer wanted to entice a number of prospects from around the country, he planned a very special open house weekend at his facility, including a celebration, golf, and some fun time. Each prospect was sent a package containing an engraved invitation, a personal letter from the CEO, an agenda that oozed with excitement, and a certificate good for two coach round-trip air tickets to Phoenix. Everything was paid for by the host. It was a huge success, and almost all the prospects flew to Phoenix. In time, they converted many of those prospects to

---

Assignment

Think of free or inexpensive things you can do that are within your budget. Get your team together and come up with some creative ideas.

---

loyal customers. There's something about show-and-tell and bricks-and-mortar that pays off, but the freebie was the real catalyst that made it work.

Epilogue

The word free *will always be the number one motivator of people, both personally and professionally.*

88

Creative Advertising Can Work

If you do any radio or television advertising, then you know it's incredibly expensive, ineffective, and often a poor use of your promotional money. But it doesn't have to be that way. You can break through the clutter, get people's attention, and build name recognition by doing something a little different. We call it problem-solving with a dose of humor.

One of the best uses of problem, solution, and humor has been an ad by the Hertz car rental company. A gentleman walks up to a shabby car rental establishment and explains he'd like to rent a Bronco. The shady

Assignment

Any time you're creating ads, whether for print or broadcast media, try to use the formula of problem, solution, and humor.

employee behind the counter quickly fills out the paper, takes his money, and the camera quickly switches to this poor guy on top of a horse bucking, kicking, and giving him a hard time. Unfortunately, he's been duped. Now the camera switches to Hertz and how they go above and beyond to deliver a real

113

Bronco (manufactured by Ford) and provide customer service like no one else. People love to be entertained, and they love to see a problem and solution, but when you tickle their funny bone they will remember you.

Epilogue

If your advertising is just like everyone else's, you'll probably get about the same results they do. Break through the clutter with a healthy dose of creativity and humor.

89

Claim Those Free Dollars

Promotion is more important than ever, and most manufacturers and distributors have funds available to help you go after those prospects you so desperately need. It's called co-op promotions. Some pay up to 90 percent of the actual cost! And you aren't limited to using the radio, TV, or print ads alone. Creativity can get that same chunk of cash transferred to your account to do things like mailings, trade shows, customer luncheons, golf outings, a fishing contest, or a weekend escape. Creativity will help you claim those free funds.

Assignment

Catalog every major brand and customer you deal with and aggressively go after any funds that might be available. Make yourself a sign that says *Claim It or Lose It*, because if you don't get those funds on a strategic basis, someone else will!

114

Harry was an aggressive retailer who loved to promote his business and go after prospects, especially with other people's money. He kept a log of every supplier and pushed every manufacturer as to what spiffs, co-ops, and promotion money was available. He would ask and ask and ask again. He was relentless. He befriended many of the sales reps who called on him and learned they had discretionary dollars. By being friendly and asking often, he got the promotional money to go out and get new customers.

> ### Epilogue
> *Remember, if you don't ask, you'll never get!*

90

One Magic Question

Everyone who wants more customers longs for a magic formula to guarantee more business. Be sure to ask them the magic question that is virtually guaranteed to bring you more business.

Dan, a now-retired lifetime prospector, has successfully sold everything from oil filters to investments in oil wells. He pioneered a three-step process that worked like magic to turn prospects into new customers. Do you want to know what the formula is? (1) Find out much as you can about your prospect on a personal level to connect and build rapport; (2) Probe, dig, and unearth what your prospect needs; and (3) When that picture is clear, ask them the magic question: "If I can find a way to provide the products and services you need, would you consider

> **Assignment**
>
> Write out Dan's 1-2-3 formula, and pay attention to the answers. Use this formula when you are prospecting for customers.

buying it from me?" This formula helped Dan sell millions of dollars of products and services in a variety of businesses and industries.

Epilogue

Many seasoned and successful salespeople claim you need to ask your way to success.

91

Prospects Must Be a M-A-N

How many times have you thought you had a prospect ready to say yes and become a first-time customer, only to be blown away by those disastrous words, "We can't afford it," or, "I have to get permission to buy it," or, "Sorry, but we don't really need it?" If you've encountered any of those deadly sales killers, then you need to make sure every prospect is a M-A-N. That stands for having the Means, the Authority, and the Need to buy.

Mary Anne had called on a manufacturing company's purchasing agent several times, and had established a good rapport. She was confident that by sticking with it, she would get their business for the industrial tools, cutting drill bits, and hand tools that they needed. Only after several months did the buyer finally explain that his wife was also a representative of an industrial tool company, and he just couldn't buy from anyone else.

Mary Anne had been going down a dead-end path because she had not qualified the prospect to make sure that he had the means, the authority, and the need to buy.

Assignment

Make sure in advance that your prospect is a fit for doing business with you. Make sure they have the means (such as the money or the credit), the authority (or the right to sign a purchasing agreement), and the need (that they truly have a use for your product or services).

Epilogue

Have you ever tried to sell clothing to a nudist, meat to vegetarians, Bibles to Atheists or guns to peace activists? If so, you know what it's like to waste your time with an unqualified prospect.

92

Yes, No, and Maybe

Nothing contributes more to the demise of salespeople and prospectors than the word "maybe." Everyone understands yes, it's time to go. Everyone understands no, it's time to quit, but the worst is when prospects string you along with the word maybe. It's somewhat like fishing, when the fish keep nibbling all day long, but you don't catch anything. At the end of the day, you have no fish, no bait, and no daylight left. You've spent your entire day waiting around for a maybe to become a no, which is just a waste of your time. Learn that maybe is not an acceptable answer.

> **Assignment**
>
> Professional prospectors often hang on too long, wasting their resources. You need to know when to quit fishing and find another lake.

Andy says he understands yes and no, but maybe is the word he's had to learn to deal with most often. After a reasonable period of time, he will do virtually anything to get the customer to move in one direction or another. He actually sees it as a benefit when someone says no, because he can take him or her off of the maybe list.

> **Epilogue**
>
> Customers will often string you along, and there is a huge benefit in getting them to say either yes or say no. Don't be afraid to take a knockout punch to find out whether it's worth investing your time and energy.

93

Bigger Is Better

If you operate a small or mid-sized business, there are probably times when your prospects need to see you as a Goliath in a land full of Davids. You need to use perception and illusion to appear bigger than you are. In many prospects' eyes, bigger is better.

Jack operates half a dozen delivery and service trucks that feature eye-catching graphics and are kept meticulously clean. His graphic designer suggested a bite-size idea that has convinced prospects he must surely be operating a large fleet of vehicles. They began numbering his trucks with different numbers on the right and left sides, because no one ever sees both sides of a truck at the same time. For example, on the front of the first truck it says Unit 6 on the left side, and Unit 8 on the right side. On the next truck, it says Unit 10 on the left and Unit 12 on the right. Then they do Units 14 and 16, 18 and 20, 22 and 24. If you see his trucks coming or going, you would believe that they have the largest fleet in town, when in reality it's an illusion because they only operate six vehicles. How can you use the same idea to look bigger to your prospects?

> ### *Assignment*
>
> Find some creative ways to make you outfit look more like Goliath than David. But be careful, most illusions are uncovered at some point.

Epilogue

Sometimes a small idea can have big results when using an illusion to build perception with your prospects.

119

94

Networking

Jack had tried several times to get past the gatekeepers and reach the president of a successful restaurant chain to talk to him about his unique flat-rate maintenance program for their commercial heating and air conditioning systems. He could offer the company a better service at a better price, but he couldn't get through to the president.

One Sunday morning at church, he overheard another parishioner mention that he knew the president of the restaurant chain. Jack approached the man and asked him if he would introduce Jack and his company to the president so he could tell him about Jack's great service. The very next morning, Jack got a call from his friend telling him that the president was expecting him to call, and would welcome setting up a meeting to discuss how Jack could help them get better service at less cost.

Assignment

Do your homework to find out who your colleagues, coworkers, friends, and family know. Almost everyone knows someone who could be a prospect.

Epilogue

Who do you know who could open a door for you?

95

One Size Fits All

One size will never fit all, and you need to see every prospect as an individual who needs a custom tailored program for their needs. Great prospectors don't have rigid policies and procedures. Instead they empower their people by giving them flexible guidelines to follow.

The more often Mary Anne called on Charlie the more often she realized he had the potential to be a high volume customer. But so far, all she had been able to get was an occasional sale. While walking into his facility one day, Mary Anne noticed a piece of equipment stuck back under a workbench that she had sold him several months before.

> ### *Assignment*
>
> Do you have rigid guidelines, rules, or regulations that you can't adjust to fit your customer's needs? Remember that one size does not fit all. Tailor everything you do to the individual buyer, and you'll win a lot of customers.

When she inquired why Charlie wasn't using it, he explained that while there was nothing wrong with the equipment, it simply didn't work for the application he needed. She immediately went over, pulled it out from under the workbench, wiped it off, and told him she was going to take it back and give him a credit. He quickly explained it wasn't her fault, and she really didn't owe him a credit, because the sales period had run out, and it was actually his fault that he bought it and didn't return it earlier. Because Mary Anne's company offered her guidelines and not hard-and-fast rules, she knew it would be smart to take the item back and give Charlie a credit. That one gesture pushed him over the edge, and he immediately became one of her highest volume buyers and a most loyal customer.

Epilogue

So many people are afraid of being taken advantage of that they fail to realize 98 percent of customers just want a fair deal, and to be treated as individuals.

96

All's Fair in Love and War

Everyone has heard the old proverb "All's fair in love and war." For this quick idea, we add a third description to that: "All's fair in love, war, and competition for customers." If you are going to compete in the marketplace, you must know what your competition is doing. There are three kinds of people who compete: (1) Those who are active; (2) Those who are reactive; and (3) Those who are inactive. Only the active will win the competitive wars in the days ahead.

If you ask Dorothy about what is going on with her competitors, she can not only tell you, she can show you. She has a file on each competitor, and she makes a daily effort to keep up with what they are doing. She has a network of informants who keep her advised and bring her catalogues, price

---

Assignment

Ask all your friends, employees, sales reps, colleagues, and industry contacts to bring you materials and keep you up to date on what the competition is doing. Be active!

---

sheets, promotional information, and the kinds of details she needs. There is no way you can have a good strategic program to get new customers unless you know what your competition is doing. If you are inactive or reactive, make a decision today to become active.

Epilogue

Fairness is in the eye of the beholder, and if it's honest and morally right, you must know what your competition is doing.

97

Do You Know What They Know?

In today's high-tech world, it is impossible to know what a prospect knows without doing some research. There are some grave dangers in making assumptions. It's dangerous to get caught up in the jargon of your product or service and assume the customer knows the language, but it's also dangerous to talk down to a client who has a great deal of industry knowledge. The best rule is to assume that you don't know, and then find out.

When a sales manager called a prospect, he began to explain his products and services in what could be called Customer Basics 101. He was dealing with the most rudimentary facts and figures. The problem was the gentleman on the other end was an engineering professor in the area of interest they were discussing. The more the sales manager talked on, the more upset the prospect became. Finally the prospect ended the call because he felt insulted and childish. A safe question is to ask is, "How familiar are you with this subject area or this

> **Assignment**
>
> Make a 3 × 5 card that simply says *Speak Their Language!* and keep it visible around your workspace as a constant reminder.

product or service, and what would be helpful for you to know?" Let the customer tell you what they want to know and then pick up the conversation from there.

Epilogue

You will rarely get in trouble when you let the customer tell you what they need to know.

98

What Gets Repeated

For this quick idea, we borrow a basic principle from personal influence psychology, which was pioneered by the late M.R. Kopmeyer. The key principle is *What Gets Rewarded Gets Repeated*. Reinforce that action with a compliment, a comment, a note, a small gift, or anything that might stimulate them to do it again. Build on the successes you have with each prospect. As you reinforce the behavior, they will do it more often.

Christy was a new executive assistant to a hospital administrator when he handed off a real mess. He asked her to take his pile of papers, notes, and scraps and turn it in to an executive report that he could turn in to the board of directors. She dug in and spent a tiresome day taking his jumbled mess and turning it into a professional report. When she left it on his desk, he came out bubbling with excitement about what she had accomplished. He told her that the next day he was buying her lunch. Christy learned that when she does well, he acknowledges and rewards her, which makes Christy want to do even more. It's a win-win situation for both of them.

Assignment

Make yourself a poster or card to remind yourself *What Gets Rewarded Gets Repeated* Build on positive behavior, and as much as possible, overlook the errors, sins, and omissions of your people and watch what happens.

Epilogue

Catching people being good means overriding our natural instinct to criticize, condemn, and complain.

99

Traditions Should Be Sacred

It is important in your prospecting efforts to communicate the traditions of your company that prospects will respect and admire. These traditions should be held sacred by you and your associates, because they embody the ideals and philosophies that your company holds. After all, everyone likes a touch of class. It can help build spirit and encourage prospects to see you and your company as one of value and substance.

On a fact-finding mission to South America, one business CEO was overwhelmed with how much the local culture respected their temples, statues, and religious beliefs. Very quickly, the executive found himself being very careful about where he stepped, where he walked, and how he handled himself. He had unconsciously adopted their respectful attitude, and found himself behaving similarly towards their culture.

> **Assignment**
> What do you hold sacred? Decide on a few things that are sacred to your company and protect them. Tell your prospects what they mean to you and what they should mean to them.

He realized that he could apply this to his own business. When he went back to his office, he worked with his staff to create a set of traditions and values that his prospects, customers, and associates could see and appreciate.

> **Epilogue**
> *Caring creates caring, and by identifying traditions within your company, people will quickly come to respect the values you hold and the principles for which you stand.*

100

The Puppy Dog Lick

Many people become dog owners as a direct result of the law of unintended consequences. At some point they picked up a warm, cuddly puppy who gave them a big, loving lick across the face, and they were sold. Without ever intending to own a pet, they suddenly found themselves a dog-owner. That puppy went home to become a part of the family.

When a suburban homeowner with several acres of beautiful woods went out to buy a chainsaw, he was really disappointed with what he found in most stores. The display saws looked cheap, were tied down, and did not appear capable of doing a tough job. Finally, he hit a home run when he stopped in a store that had a huge display of

> **Assignment**
>
> Get your prospects to try out your product or service. Offer free on-sites tests of your products, free 15-day trials of your services, or anything else you can think of to get them to try your company. If they try it, they'll most likely buy it.

chainsaws and people who could explain about each and every one. But the puppy dog lick came when the sales rep invited him to go out back with the chainsaw and try it out. After cutting several limbs from a tree trunk they used as a testing site, he was sold. They made a sale, and everyone else lost out on a prospect that day.

Epilogue

All the advertising in the world can't compare to one good personal experience.

101

Don't Give Them a Reason

Have you ever met someone who wouldn't change their mind or wouldn't change the subject? That is the exact principle one highly successful entrepreneur used in building a number of profitable businesses. His philosophy was, "Never give a customer a reason to go somewhere else."

It was just a few minutes after 6 a.m. as customers began to enter a local bakery and espresso bar. To their great dismay, they were greeted with an announcement that the coffee and bread store had no coffee. They had run out, and therefore, customers had to drink soda or water, or go somewhere else. Many of them went out the door and down the street to a nearby shop that had coffee. Unbelievably, there was a 24-hour supermarket just a few blocks away where the store employees could have gotten a variety of coffees and met their customers' needs. They literally forced their regular customers to go elsewhere for that first cup of coffee. This is industrial strength stupidity.

> ### Assignment
>
> The goal is to become the competition, and never send your customers elsewhere for the things you should have.

Epilogue

If your customer goes somewhere else three times, they're probably going to like them better.

102

What Is It You Sell?

When Jack Trout and Al Reis wrote the popular book, *Positioning: The Battle for Your Mind*, they said that your business name is crucial. It should be the shortest distance between you and your prospect's mind. Review these actual business names, and try to tell me what these people sell: Tuesday Morning, A.J.'s Closet, 21st Amendment, The Sugar Plum Tree, Bounce Back, Tulip Tree, Priscilla's, Mad Dog's Place, Amerispec, and Juniper Services. My bet is if you hit even one or two, it would be a miracle. Does your business name really tell who you are and what you do? If not, maybe it's time to change.

Assignment

If you can't change your business name, consider working hard to define the tag line below your name that tells what you do and why customers should come to you.

Epilogue

It is time to put your ego aside and decide that the most important thing you have is the name of your business.

129

103

Everything Matters

What's important to that new customer you've been trying to win over from your competitor? Everything! Getting new customers is about doing a few big things, and hundreds of small things, better than your competition. We call it managing your T-C-E, or the Total Customer Experience.

Picture yourself in a gymnastics competition where at the end of a performance, the judges hold up their scorecards. You will see things like 9.1, 9.4, and 9.7. But it's the cumulative score that will determine the

> **Assignment**
>
> Pay attention to the details, not just the major elements of your business.

final rank for that gymnast. It's the same way with your company. You have to be concerned with a few big things, and hundreds of little things. It's the attention to detail that will ultimately win over your customers. Customers know they have options and choices, and if you don't manage your T-C-E, they might go somewhere else.

Epilogue

Getting new customers is a matter of doing a better job of managing your Total Customer Experience.

104

When Do You Need It?

While giving a guided tour of his Phoenix-based promotional item company, Jim was explaining how deadlines have changed, and how much faster our lives move. Just a decade ago he said an order would come in for custom printed items like business cards or coffee mugs, and his company would be excited if they could complete the order and ship it back to the customer in ten days. Today, these orders often come in with the first mail at 8 a.m., and are finished and headed out of the plant by 10 a.m. It's a fast-paced world.

One of the secrets to meeting and exceeding your deadlines is not telling them when you can do something for them, but asking them when they would like to have it. You have to understand their timeframe. Oftentimes their deadline may not be nearly as soon or as critical

Assignment

Work first to get their ideal deadline, and then if necessary, you can negotiate on the actual deadline with which you both can live.

as you think. They may need something in a week, but you thought they would want it in a day. There are two main benefits that come from properly assessing a customer's needs. The first is the opportunity to exceed their expectation and get it there more quickly than needed. The second is to schedule your work and your production to meet their needs, not yours.

Epilogue
In today's fast-paced world, the ongoing practice of under-promise and over-deliver will win you more customers than you can possibly imagine.

105

Lost Sales Mean Opportunities

Lost sales, special orders, and buyouts can be an opportunity to businesses that have the right inventories and are paying attention to what their customers want and need. When one small store started keeping records of special purchases and items on which they lost sales, they quickly found one particular item they had reordered five times for a customer, and it was an item they didn't stock. When this business offered to stock the customer's special needs, the customer assured them that they would get all their business. By tracking just one special purchase, they ended up with a profitable new account. What are you doing to keep track of items you don't have, and to analyze those special orders and lost sales?

> ### *Assignment*
> Keep your inventory up to date, and track all your orders. The goal is to always have what you should have, and never have what you shouldn't have.

Epilogue

Anyone can say, "No, we don't have it." But it's the people who can say "We'll get it," who consistently win over the new customers.

106

Let Them Decide

There is no way to estimate a customer's willingness to spend money on repairs, improvements, products, or services they really want. Never tell a customer how they should invest their money. Let them make the decision. Don't throw cold water on a possible sale when you don't know the value of the item or transaction they are considering. Oftentimes sentimental value, emotions, and history play into a customer's decision to spend more than you might think makes sense.

> **Assignment**
>
> Value is in the eye of the beholder. Put the customer in the power position, give them their options, and then let them make the decision.

When the owner of a high-rise office building in downtown Chicago attempted to sell the building, it had fallen into disrepair and was completely vacant. When one prospect came in, he began to belittle the value of the building as he talked about the leaky roof, the loose brick, and other major repairs. There was no way for the existing owner to know how much or how badly this prospect wanted to own the building. The more the prospect talked the building down, the more the existing owner lowered the price. Finally they reached a deal, and unexpectedly the new owner had the building imploded and removed from the site. He knew the value of the land, which was what he really wanted. The seller lost thousands of dollars because he assumed the buyer wanted the building, not the land.

Epilogue

Your job is to inform prospects of their options, and their job is to decide what best fits them and their budgets, needs, and wants.

107

Forget Satisfied

In years past, the goal of businesses was to satisfy their customers. Everyone thought that satisfy was the key word, and that it was a sure-fire formula to foster relationships, encourage customer loyalty, and build repeat business. Now we know that it's not enough. Businesses must raise the bar, and strive to go from good to great, and "delight" their customers.

The University of Michigan monitors customer satisfaction, and rates business successes as it relates to customer satisfaction. Some researchers credit more demanding and better-informed customers as the driving force behind the move from satisfied to delighted. What does this mean for you? You've got to rethink, rework, and realign your goals, systems, procedures, and training. You have to find the

Assignment

Delighted customers come from service as much as product. Make a sign for your office/service area. On the sign put the word *Satisfied* then cross it out and write over it *Delighted*. Use this poster to remind everyone that the new standard is delighted.

strategies and tactics that yield an outcome of delighted customers, and adjust your practices accordingly.

Epilogue

The primary reason satisfied doesn't work anymore is because that's what customers believe they hired you to do originally, and all you're doing is fulfilling the agreement they made with you when they made a purchase. Delighted however, goes above and beyond their expectations.

108

Perceptions of Value

In prospecting today, we often throw around terminology that does not have supporting facts and figures. Unique selling position, economies of scale, service philosophy, and brand promise are all examples of words that require more information before they can be used effectively. It's amazing how most companies assume, and make poorly informed judgments, about how their prospects and customers perceive value of goods and services.

At Tuckman Cleaners, a sign hangs from the ceiling

Assignment

Don't operate in the dark. Conduct surveys and get a true grasp on how your customers view you and perceive the value you are providing. Then communicate that value to your prospects, so they can become loyal customers too!

---

of each location that says "The Only Opinion of Value that Counts is Our Customers' Perception of Value."

Epilogue

Regardless of the words, terms, and phrases you use, at the end of the day, customers buy value.

109

Prospecting With Hulk and Bulk

Greg runs a farm equipment dealership where John Deere is their primary product line. Driving by Greg's store in season is an experience. You will see riding mowers and lawn equipment in huge stacks higher than their building. Out front you will see dozens of tractors, trailers, front-loaders, and other heavy equipment lined up ready for delivery. Their displays, which use hulk and bulk, is one of the key reasons Greg's store is one of the largest in the region. Don't overlook the power of hulk and bulk to send a message to your prospects that you are an expert, you are serious, and you can be trusted to have what they want.

Assignment

Borrow from the *hulk and bulk* principle. When you advertise, show lots of the product. Put it by the doors, in the aisles, or at the checkout counter. Focus on two or three items that will attract customers, and overwhelm them with quantity.

> ### Epilogue
>
> *Perhaps the greatest payoff of the hulk and bulk principle is that it establishes a visual memory connecting your company with a specific item. So when the customer needs it tomorrow, they will remember you today.*

110

It's All About Value

If you want to get your coworkers to see the value of a prospect, talk to them in terms of a customer's annual spending and how much they could be worth over a lifetime. It gives your employees and staff an entirely new perspective on that prospective customer. For example, one executive found that his average member contributed $550 in gross profit to his association each year, and that the average member stayed a total of 6 1/2 years on their membership roster. That adds up to $3,575 per customer! The association quickly learned they could really invest in landing that prospect. In fact, they could afford to spend an entire year's profit on recruitment because they would make it up in the long-term.

> ### Assignment
>
> Teach your associates the value of long-term customers. You can delight your long-term customers by doing extra little things to show your appreciation. Enhance the value of your business by adding extra benefits.

> **Epilogue**
>
> *Teach your people that every prospect has the potential to be a big spender, and should be treated accordingly.*

111

How Much Does It Cost?

One retailer had a 300-piece tool rack, and noticed that customers would spin the rack, pick items up, look them over, but then put them back and walk out the door. He believed the problem was that there weren't prices on the items, and people were too timid, too busy, or just not interested enough to ask. So he tried an experiment. He put a price tag on all 300 items. Instantly, sales increased 40 percent. Could simply having a price on the merchandise increase sales that much? There was only one way to find out. He went back and carefully removed all 300 price stickers and tracked sales for the next 60 days. Amazingly, sales went right back to the previous level. He proved that everything has to be priced, or customers will see it as value-less and simply walk away.

> **Assignment**
>
> Many people are too timid or feel they will be obligated if they ask the price. Do a daily sweep of your facility to make sure everything has a price so customers won't see it as value-less.

138

Epilogue

Customers will not ask for a price because they expect it to be there. If it's not, you are violating their expectations and they'll probably take a hike.

112

Stack Up the Benefits

When you talk about the features of your product or service, be sure to explain the benefits. Here are three good phrases you can use: (1) "What that means to you is..."; (2) "That is important to know because..."; or (3) "You will love this, because it will help you...."

For example, when you buy a drill, what are you really purchasing? The drill? The bit? Nope. You want to be able to take that drill and make a hole. Being able to make a hole is the benefit of the tool, and is really what you are purchasing from the hardware store. It is so easy to get caught up in talking about the features of your products that you overlook the real benefits. And at the end of the day, customers want to buy benefits.

Assignment

When you learn to be great at communicating both features and benefits, your prospects will see that you are really selling value, and they want to become your customer.

Epilogue

At the end of the day, people don't buy what products are, they buy what that product will do.

113

What You Can Do

It is so easy to see the negatives in life, and completely miss the positives. It's easy to see the ruts in the road instead of the beautiful highway. As you hunt for new customers, it's guaranteed that you will find a competitor who is bigger, better, and more established, who will present a real challenge for you. The secret is to focus on what you can do, without over-looking what you can't do.

Herb worked in a small company where they had three sales representatives. He was the author of doom and gloom. If the company asked him to work a special price promotion, you can bet he would say the price was too high. If they took on a new product line, he would whine and complain that it

> **Assignment**
>
> Keep yourself and your sales team focused on the positive. Maintain that by showing your associates your own positive attitude. Always have three positive things to say to the team.

was the wrong brand. Herb dragged the other people in the company down so much that management decided to invite him to work somewhere else. Are you focused on the positives or the negatives in your attempts to get new customers?

Epilogue

Remember that the glass is always half full.

114

How Much Is Your Price?

If you pick up the Sunday newspaper, you will see lots of flyers and inserts promoting low prices. Or if you walk through the mall, look at all the signs for sales, promotions, and great deals. Most merchants make price their key selling issue. You need to be aware that when you cave in to price, you may be giving money away. While price is important, it is never at the top of the list for most buyers. Standing your ground to sell value may have a bigger pay-off than lowering your price.

There are only two types of buyers in the world. First is the price-based buyer, who is trying to get the best deal they for every purchase. The second type of buyer is the value-based buyer. They want to know what they're going to get for their money.

Assignment

Have all your employees write out why you are justified in your pricing, features, benefits, and guarantees on all your major products or services.

If both of these buyers are smart, they will ask you about price. The price buyer is testing you to see if you will come down, and the value buyer is testing you to see if you really believe in your price and product. If you sell on value, one of the great responses when people ask about the price is to say, "Yes, the price is..." and give them the amount, and then tell them, "And I'm as surprised as you are that we can afford to sell for that. May I explain to you why you'd be smart to invest your money in this?" These key phrases can help you overcome that price barrier, but the main thing is for you to stand firm and believe that what you're selling is worth what you're asking. If you don't believe in your product, you will never convince the buyer to either.

Epilogue

The easiest selling method in the world is to cave in and lower the price, which means you are giving away money. Are you sure that's what you want to do?

115

The $10 Stupidity

Have you noticed how many businesses run expensive ads, offer deep discounts, coupons, giveaways, and all kinds of enticements to get you to buy? But when it comes time to take your money, they can't do it? They have lines backed up, people who aren't properly trained, or people who have no customer service experience. An additional person or a little more training could fix this problem, and make a bad experience a pleasurable one for as little as $10 an hour.

Assignment

Human beings are creatures of habit, and are always going to take the path of least resistance. Analyze your procedures and make it easy for the customer to buy.

When it comes time to getting the customer to say yes, don't be guilty of a $10 stupidity. Hire that extra staff, train your current associates, or invest in that extra piece of machinery that will make working under pressure much simpler. Work to make it easy, enjoyable, and quick, because if you are not ready when the customer is finally willing to hand over the cash, you're in big trouble.

Epilogue

Make it a goal to have the right people, with the right training, the right attitude, and in the right quantity at the right time, and you'll turn prospects into buying customers more than ever before.

116

Losing Their Luster

Coupons, discounts, and promotions are so overused today, they are no longer an effective motivator to get new customers and boost sales. For example, almost every supermarket has overpriced their merchandise. To get it reduced to the price you should pay, you have to carry one of their frequent buyer cards. Consider a different approach by using premiums, gifts, and other incentives to get customers to do business with you.

When one of my friends bought a painfully overpriced luxury SUV, he nearly got into a fight with the sales manager when they refused to give him the free cap and jacket that his golfing buddies had gotten when they bought the same car. Don't lose sight of the fact that some of the most unique incentives have spurred people to switch suppliers and become customers when coupons and discounts probably had little meaning to them. Begin today to experiment with what motivates your customers to go the extra mile.

Epilogue

People make emotional decisions about what they buy and where they buy, but they like to justify their purchases with logical explanations.

117

Tell Them What You Can Do

No driver likes to end up on a dead-end street, and no businessperson enjoys being left in a bad situation by a supplier. Develop a reputation for caring, trying, and helping. Anytime you have to tell a customer what you can't do, also tell them what you can do. Always have the information available to offer your customers an alternative if you are not able to meet

> ## Assignment
>
> Identify the top 10 times when you are forced to say no. Develop a few potential positive responses that can be partnered with the no's. For example, when you have to tell a prospect that you can't get their order in time, be sure to say that you can give them a 20 percent discount.

their needs. Make sure that there are no dead-ends if they deal with you.

In the well-known movie *Miracle on 34th Street*, Santa Claus made this principle work for him during the busy Christmas shopping season. When a child sat on his lap and asked for a toy that Santa didn't have he directed the child's parents to a competitor in the area. The parents were so amazed with Santa's behavior, they came back to his store and brought all their friends and family as well.

> ### Epilogue
>
> *Anyone can say no, sorry, or tough luck. But you will earn the respect and business of potential customers when you help them by telling them what you can do. Balance the negative with the positive, and be sure to give the customer options.*

118

Are You Listening?

Walter, a veteran sales rep, had a legendary reputation for talking, and a costly reputation for not listening. On one sales call alone, a manufacturer's rep working with him picked up on three huge buying signals from the prospect, while Walter never even slowed down. He kept talking, even though the customer had heard everything he needed to hear. Because Walter didn't take the time to listen to his customer, they left without having made the sale.

Great companies develop great people who know how to really listen. The problem is, most prospecting conversations aren't about talking and listening; they are about two people just waiting for the other to stop talking. Most prospects will drop buying signals when they're ready to close the deal. It's your job to make sure you can hear them!

Assignment

Talk only 1/3 of the time you are with a prospect. If they don't talk, ask questions. Train yourself and your team to listen. After all, it's the customer's needs, not yours, that need to be satisfied. Give them a chance to express their needs.

Epilogue

Listening requires practice, dedication, and discipline.

119

The Early Bird Gets the New Customer

Staying on the cutting edge of changes, new products, services, and new technologies is a must if you want to be perceived as the best resource for prospects and customers. It takes real work and a commitment from everyone to keep up with all the changes in our world today.

Assignment

Make it a point to be the most informed and up to date in your industry. Provide your staff with the tools and insist they use them. Make your sales staff the people with the latest information about your industry. Your customers and prospects will learn that you can be depended on to have the most up-to-date information in the industry.

Tom operates a group of successful retail stores spread across Iowa and Wisconsin. He believes one of their marketing advantages comes from making a major effort to monitor the industry for new information and changes that are happening in their marketplace. To keep up, he and his crew receive a variety of trade publications each month. They are always walking the aisles of trade shows and manufacturers' exhibits, and they carefully monitor manufacturers' mailings to see what is new. They also invest in several newsletters, including a daily fax bulletin that keeps them informed of what is going on in their market. His salespeople frequently know days, weeks, and sometimes months in advance, long before their competition even gets wind of what

147

is going on. They are perceived as the best resource to offer customers the information and products they need.

Epilogue

Our world is changing by the second, and if you don't change with it, you'll be listed in the book, "Who's Through," in your business category.

120

The Problem With Communication

In prospecting for new customers, effective communication can be incredible challenging. So much of what we do is verbal, and sometimes we forget that other kinds of communication can be just as effective. Don't forget that visual communication can play a big part in prospecting for new customers.

Herb was a white-haired manager, and he called that white hair his frost of wisdom. One of his favorite reminders was how dangerous verbal orders could be. In fact, he said communication problems normally come from one of three areas: (1) There was no communication in the first place; (2) We misspoke or misunderstood the original communication;

Assignment

Create a backup system using e-mail, voice mail, or written orders to make sure that there are no verbal orders that are misunderstood. Especially when they are orders from customers or requests for information from prospects!

or (3) We assumed we had the answer, and went ahead without confirming the information. Herb had a bright yellow form that he insisted everyone use. It said *Avoid Verbal Orders* in big, bold letters across the top, and it said *Put It In Writing* along the bottom. What are you doing to make sure you communicate effectively within your organization and with your prospects?

Epilogue

Remember that the message is always in the mind of the receiver, and by putting it in writing, you vastly increase the likelihood the message will be communicated correctly.

121

No Is Not the Answer

Fear is the greatest single challenge that you must overcome if you're going to be successful at turning prospects into customers. When many salespeople hear the word "no," they give up or give in. But if you are going to succeed in prospecting for customers, you can't quit when you hear the word no. You've got to step back, look at the situation, and try to find a new approach to get your prospects to say "yes."

Ron was a bright, young salesperson for a company in Chicago. He was organized, well-groomed, and articulate, and kept great records about his sales prospecting. The only problem was that he wasn't getting new business, and no one in his company could figure out why. Finally they hired a sales consultant who traveled with Ron and critiqued his selling style. What they found is that when a customer said no, Ron quit and simply gave up. He was giving in and giving up instead of finding ways to overcome the no and change it to a yes. Winston Churchill said, "It is not enough that we do our best. Sometimes we have to do what's required."

Assignment

Don't quit when you hear the word "no." Take a step back and think about what you tried, and then try something different. You've got to keep going until you can change a "no" into a "yes."

Epilogue

You're not defeated until you give up. The moment you say, "I quit," you have defeated yourself.

122

Selective Hearing

You need to beware of promises, claims, or even casual comments. Customers have selective hearing and selective memory, and you can bet they will remember in a way that suits them best! If you tell them you can get it in a week, they'll be calling you in three days wanting to know where it is. If you tell them you think you can get it for free, they'll want to know how much you're going to pay them to take it. And if you say you can do something and then you have to renege, your chances of getting that customer to come back to you are very slim.

When Betty, a financial services representative, called on a potential broker, she told them she was pretty certain that she

Assignment

When you make statements or promises that might be interpreted by a prospect or customer as certain, remind them "if it ain't in writing, it ain't so." Then, when you know you can make such a promise, put it in writing for them.

could get a promotional package for them at little or no cost. Those words came back to haunt her. On the very next prospecting call, the client wanted to know where that complete promotional package was that she promised to get them for free. What she quickly learned was that a casual comment can be turned to her disadvantage.

Epilogue

Some people will lie, and some people truly have selective hearing. Regardless, they will try to use your words against you.

123

If Only We Had Time

My grandfather used to say that both meetings and sermons should end on the same day they began. He was a nut about wasting time. He recognized that there are only 24 hours in a day, so it's important to spend those hours wisely. It's vital to recognize the value of a customer's time, especially when they are investing that time in listening to you. The pressure on business people today to get more done in less time is the biggest complaint by business owners and associates today.

Michael, an award-winning sales rep, follows the Vince Lombardi rule. If he's not 10 minutes early for an appointment with a prospect or customer, he feels like he is late. He believes a great deal of his success, and his foundation for being a salesman, is his

> ## *Assignment*
> Make managing your time a critical ingredient of your prospecting, and let customers know what your expectations are up front.

respect for other people's time. Three of his rules are: (1) Always be on time or early for your commitments; (2) Always be prepared with no fumbling, excuses, or stories; and (3) Always end at the time you promised, and remind a customer or prospect of how much you value their time. Are you always early, prepared, and respectful of other people's time? If not, it may be a real stumbling block to getting the new customers you want.

> ### Epilogue
> *The phrase "time-management" is really a misnomer. You're not trying to manage your time, you're actually trying to manage your life to fit into the existing and unchanging time. Ultimately, you have to respect your prospect's time, and they will respect you.*

124

Anticipate Obstacles

Author John Newborn said, "People can be divided into three groups: those who make things happen, those who watch things happen, and those who wonder what happened." This certainly applies to people in business, particularly on the subject of gaining and retaining customers. The secret to your success is to ask yourself which group you're in. An even better question is to ask to which group you want to belong.

Prominent author and business leader Frank Basile says that when he teaches goal-setting, he teaches to be goal oriented people. An important ingredient of his goal-setting training is to anticipate that there will be obstacles ahead that will have to be handled to reach those goals. He says to take the word "try" out of your vocabulary, because it sets you up for failure and excuses. Would you want to fly with a pilot who is going to "try" to land safely? What you need to do when you set a goal is say to yourself, "I'm going to make this happen," and then get it done.

Assignment

Become a goal-oriented manager, especially when it comes to getting new customers.

> ### Epilogue
> *One seasoned sales manager said he only has two kinds of people: (1) Those who make a quota, and (2) Those who make excuses.*

153

125

Decide Not to Sell

Many amateur salespeople think every sales call must be an attempt to make a sale. Experienced professionals know that oftentimes there is a great deal of research, investigation, and diagnosis necessary before they can possibly think about closing the deal.

The owner of a service company was really nice to the salesperson each time she stopped by. However, he claimed he was getting the best price, the best delivery, and the best inventory management when he bought

Assignment

Probe, look, and listen. Be patient. Find your competitive advantages before trying to make the sale.

from someone else. It took her more than six months to develop the big picture and to learn that most of what he claimed wasn't true. In fact, many of the suppliers were taking advantage of him, and he wasn't paying enough attention. He had items that should have been returned, he had merchandise left over on which he would never get his money back, and he had warranties that should have been credited long ago. After six months, this savvy salesperson finally made a case. She presented it to the owner and clearly demonstrated that her total service package was better. He immediately went from the prospect column to the customer column.

Epilogue
Remember that the goal of a sale may be not to sell at all, but simply to gather critical information.

126

Selling to the Senses

People still need to see and touch before they buy. While the Internet has proven to be a great tool for people to educate themselves, it has not measured up in terms of generating business and replacing bricks-and-mortar retailers. Take a lesson from the Big Box stores, and let your customer see and touch your merchandise.

Assignment

What do you need to put out so your people can see and touch to build a following of loyal customers? Never underestimate the value of the five senses, and try to arrange your merchandise in a manner that appeals to more than just sight.

F.W. Woolworth made a fortune when he invented the five-and-dime store. He moved the merchandise down from the high shelves and out from under the counter to where people could experience it for themselves. He taught the principle that you need to put it out where people can see it, feel it, and handle it, if you're going to successfully sell it.

Epilogue

Don't be afraid to let customers use and abuse your displays and samples, because they are great tools for turning shoppers into buyers, and prospects into customers.

127

Never Assume It Took Place

One of the most dangerous things you can do in prospecting for customers is to assume that true communication took place. We get so many magazines, letters, e-mail, direct mail, and personal mail that it's easy for important details to slip through the cracks. Bullet-proof your communications by having another set of eyes test what you are doing.

Elaine is an office assistant in a busy secretarial group. She has an uncanny ability to read and review materials to see if all the necessary details are there and to identify any communication gaps. In her office they call it the "Elaine test." With any new creative piece, including flyers, invitations, ads, and particularly events where people are invited and need to know a great deal of detail, the rule is "Give it to Elaine." If after reading it, she can tell you the details about what is happening, then it's clear and concise. If Elaine can't relate the details about what is on the agenda, then it is a clear indicator that the piece needs to be revised.

Assignment

Always check critical items going out to prospects by having a second set of eyes review the materials. Develop a system so that every item that goes out the door is double-checked for consistency and clarity. This type of proofing can catch a problem before it begins.

Epilogue

Find someone in your office or group who can function like Elaine.

128

Attention to Detail

One thing prospects quickly notice and grow to admire is a representative who dots the *i*'s and crosses the *t*'s. By paying attention to the big things and the little details, they will quickly see that you are a person on whom they can depend. Don't ever let the big picture overwhelm your vision of success.

> ### Assignment
>
> Make yourself a card with that test. Simply write down *Who, What, When, Where, Why, and How much?* Pull it out anytime you want to test something to see if it is clear and complete.

The United States military is one of the most reliable organizations in the world, and they run a test on anything and everything they do. Before running any missions or engaging in any activity, they always try to answer the following questions *Who, What, When, Where, Why, and How much?* These six ideas will give you a fairly complete idea of the task at hand, and will allow you to provide the pertinent information to your prospects. It's a test that you should use for every project and every assignment. You will never fail by giving too much attention to detail.

> ### Epilogue
>
> *If you learn to inspect what you expect, you will soon get what you want from the world of big business.*

129

Use Your Design

A really great prospector maintains a constantly updated list of great ideas to improve their prospecting efforts. One key question you should always ask yourself is, "How can I multiply my prospecting efforts without investing in more manpower?" One answer is to work on the visibility of your vehicles, and maintain top-of-mind-awareness with your prospects.

Even small and mid-sized businesses with little or no budget can benefit from carving out a unique image for their vehicles, whether they have one or 100. Think about how quickly you recognize a black and white police car, an emergency vehicle, or a simple but effective yellow cab. If you

> ### *Assignment*
> Investigate graphic design options and consider an entirely new way to identify your vehicles. Your goal is to catch people's attention and tell who you are, what you do, and how to contact you.

have a bigger budget, consider how UPS has turned thousands and thousands of ugly brown trucks into a status symbol and an internationally known logo. All these icons have been developed as a result of intent, purpose, and design. Look at your company and see what unique factors you can capitalize on to enhance your visibility.

> ### Epilogue
> *Steal, don't invent, your success. By seeing what successful people do and doing something similar to what they do, you too will be successful.*

130

Make Smiles Zero Tolerance

There are only two kinds of people to work with if you're going to win the hearts of new customers: (1) Those who should work for you; and (2) Those who should never work for you. The difference between the two is sometimes hard to identify, but I'll give you a secret. It's all about the smile!

> ### *Assignment*
> Develop your own smile testing. Let people try the job, and watch their facial expression. It will tell you everything you need to know about the person's future with your company.

Across Japan, fast food menus look just like those here in the United States: hamburgers, fries, and soft drinks. The one major difference is at the lower right-hand corner, where it almost always says "Smiles are Zero Yen." The bright attitude and good customer service skills are free of charge, and are usually the reason customers return to a specific restaurant when all the menus are the same. When you hire new employees, make it a goal to hire only those applicants who have a big smile.

> ### Epilogue
> *Even the grumpiest prospect alive wants to deal with someone who has a smile. Make sure that person is from your organization.*

131

It's Okay to Know You Don't Know

Call it ego, pride, or vanity, but however you label it, Americans are hesitant to admit when they don't know something. The really smart person knows it is okay not to know, and spends their time and effort on finding the answer. Train your employees to ask for information if they don't know the answer, rather than lie or dismiss a customer request.

Raymond drove nearly 50 miles to a computer store because he needed a highly technical part. When Raymond asked, "Are you sure this will do the job," the sales clerk responded, "I think so." That immediately set off Raymond's built-in lie detector. He exited the store and headed to a competitor,

> ### Assignment
> When you know you don't know, admit it, and find someone who does. That should be a company policy. Otherwise you drive away potential customers.

where he found a reliable answer to his question. Raymond believed it was okay not to know the answer, as long as they were willing to get someone who does.

> ### Epilogue
> *Ignorance is simply not knowing, but stupidity is claiming to know something when you don't.*

132

Don't Be a Bungling Bob

Dale Carnegie taught that selling is about relationships, and 15 percent is about what you know, and 85 percent is about who you know. While that principle is simple, it is also problematic. If you don't know the 15 percent about your products and services, it will ruin your credibility with prospects.

Each month, Bob's warehouse produced a Top 10 list of their specials for the month, and each month, Bob's customers would ask him about those specials, and Bob would have to go out to the car and search through piles of paper to find the special flyers for the month. He would bring them in, rumpled and covered with coffee stains, and sit down and read them to his prospects. Finally, one of his prospects said, "Bob, I've given you a nickname, Bungling Bob, because you don't seem to care enough to even learn about your own products and services. You also insult me, because I can read those materials by myself." Bob got a huge dose of the truth that day, and has since tried to treat his customers with dignity and respect. He makes sure that his materials are neat and organized, and he's arranged to have his special flyers mailed directly to his customers.

> **Assignment**
>
> Make it a rule each month to read your primary sales materials, bulletins, and promotions so you know in advance how to answer a prospect's questions. Also, be sure to provide the materials to your prospects directly. Don't be a Bungling Bob and indirectly sabotage your customer service.

Epilogue
When your prospects find out that you don't know, they'll think you don't really care about them and they won't deal with you.

133

Create Your Personal Gold Mine

Do you know what is more worthless than yesterday's newspaper, week-old bread, or a five-year-old phonebook? It's a database that isn't accurate. Your future success in winning over new customers will be determined largely by the quality and quantity of your prospect list. Today is the best opportunity you will ever have to make a commitment to keep that list up to date, accurate, and on target.

Early on, Joanne realized how powerful and accurate a well-maintained, up-to-date list of prospects can be. She made a commitment to do several things to keep that database accurate. First, she decided that any time she was notified of a change by people in her company, she would pick up the telephone and verify the information with the prospect. Second, she alerted coworkers in her company to pass along any information they got about changes in a prospect situation. This included people, phone numbers, or addresses. Third, on all mailings to prospects, she put the term

> ### Assignment
> Create a form that everyone can use to notify you when changes come about, and have it by their phones or desk so they can pass it along.

"Address Correction Requested" below their return address in the upper left-hand corner. That signals the post office to alert you when there's a change, and to furnish you with that information. If you're going to keep your database accurate, it is essential to have a multi-strategic approach to gaining and maintaining good information.

Epilogue

If you invest in taking care of your future customer database, your future customer database will take care of you.

134

The Insanity Principle

Albert Einstein formulated something that he called the insanity principle. The principle says you cannot continue to do the same thing many times over and expect to get a different outcome.

In one year, a sales professional made over 600 cold calls on 600 different businesses. On each call he slowly but surely conquered his fear of the unknown. On every cold call he had two questions he asked himself: (1) What should have I done differently on that sales call?

Assignment

Borrow from this professional and record the answers to those two questions each time you make a cold call. Create a diary of these responses. Then study the responses and try different approaches based on your own observations.

and (2) What should I have said differently on that call? After each of those events, he would write out what he wanted to do and say differently, and then reread the 10 most recent calls, and on the next cold call, he would try to tweak it and make it just a little different until he got a better reception.

Epilogue

Learn completely from every experience and use that learning to improve subsequent customer calls.

135

Beware of Fatal Ruts

The only difference between a rut and a grave is that a rut is a grave with the ends knocked out. It is easy to fall into a rut and take customers for granted. Any presentations you give will come off as though you were a parrot, simply repeating it again and again. Each time you give a presentation to a prospective customer, pretend you are doing it for the very first time. Get involved, watch the key points, ask the right questions and walk them through it, because they are seeing it with brandnew, fresh eyes. Don't come off like a parrot.

Assignment

Prepare every presentation as though it were the first time you've done it. Sometimes it's just a matter of putting on your game face. Prospects and customers can tell when they are not getting your best effort.

> ### Epilogue
> *If you don't make a presentation that sends a message that you care, your prospect will get a message that you don't care.*

136

Ask for Help

There's something magical that happens when you call on customers accompanied by a specialist. It's interesting how prospects, who previously wouldn't give you the time of day, will suddenly stop and listen to a person they see as an authority. Don't be afraid to reach out and get help from manufacturers, distributors, and retailers who can help you win over prospects.

> ### Assignment
> Make a list of all the people who might be able to help you, then ask their help, and make some calls. You'll be surprised how supportive your allies will be and how effective you'll become.

Examine your marketplace and ask yourself who could help you. Then when help is available, knock on the doors of those prospects who might not have given you the time of day in the past, introduce your specialists, and see what happens. It's something about having that second person traveling with you that seems to open locked doors. It might be uncomfortable or awkward, but it's always productive. Don't be afraid to ask for help.

> **Epilogue**
> When we put pride aside and ask for help, magical things can happen.

137

Criticize, Condemn, and Complain

Your attitude will be the number one ingredient in your ability to get new customers. Have you heard this quote, "Any fool can criticize, condemn, and complain, and most of them do?" Your success in business means you will not be allowed to pick the personality of the people with whom you work. It's not who you encounter that will determine your success, but how you respond to the people you encounter that will make the difference.

There are three things experienced professionals will tell you to do when you encounter someone who criticizes, condemns, or complains: (1) Beware and monitor your own words so that you don't get caught up in their negativity. You create a downward spiral that can destroy both of you; (2) Don't chime in and comment on their negatives, because you will only perpetuate them. Oftentimes, they're

> **Assignment**
> Each day pick three positive things you can talk about. If it's raining, point out how that can help grow corn. If it's cold, point out how that will create jobs, because people might need to buy coats. If the wind's blowing, talk about how that will generate power at the new windmills around the country.

testing you; and (3) When appropriate, change the subject to something positive. Get them in an upbeat mood, and everyone will be happier.

> ### Epilogue
> *A real professional never chimes in when people criticize, condemn, or complain.*

138

Harness the Internet

There's no better resource to keep you up-to-date on research, facts, figures, what competitors are doing, and what's on the horizon for your business, than learning to harness the Internet. By using the Internet to research, you can prepare to win customers to your way of business. You can find anything from how to raise fishing worms to a protocol for flying the United States flag. Instantly available are statistics on the population in your area, and a record of births and deaths. If you're not using the Internet, you're not resolving the ignorance problem. You can outsmart and outpace your competition by using the Internet as your research vehicle.

> ### *Assignment*
>
> Teach everyone to use the Internet, and make doing research a must when trying to turn prospects into customers.

> **Epilogue**
>
> When you fail to do your homework and necessary research, you're simply giving your competition an advantage over you. Why would you want to do that?

139

Tell the Truth

Most businesspeople know the difference between right and wrong, and they know the difference between honesty and deception. But there are still people who operate in shades of gray and convince themselves that it is okay to deceive, manipulate, and play with the truth to get new customers. An attitude of telling the truth, the whole truth, and nothing but the truth will work for you in the long term.

How would you feel if you bought gold from a company based on an ad that read, "Analysts predict the price of gold could double in the future." While that prediction is not illegal (although

> **Assignment**
>
> Use this as an advertising test: Is this true, and will people believe it?

it probably should be) it sure smacks of an attempt to convince buyers that gold is a sure thing, and that buying from them will give them a great return and riches untold. But it's deceptive. Yes, gold *could* double in the future, but who knows when, and who will guarantee it?

```
┌─────────────────────────────────────────────────┐
│                   Epilogue                        │
│   You will never get in trouble trying to attract │
│ customers by telling the truth, the whole truth,  │
│ and nothing but the truth.                        │
└─────────────────────────────────────────────────┘
```

140

How Are You Really Doing?

One sure test of your ability to attract more customers is to ask how you are doing with the customers you already have. Most businesses rarely ask, thinking that a lack of complaints means everyone is happy. The reality is that you will only hear from two types of customers, those who love you, and those who are unhappy with you. The killer is the great silent majority who don't whine or complain. They just quietly leave you for a competitor.

Assignment

You've got to have a system to consistently invite customers to sound off if you're going to know how your services rate. That way you can attract and retain the prospects you want.

When a salesman asked Bob how his company was doing at making their deliveries to Bob's mechanical repair department, the salesman was flabbergasted to learn that Bob thought their service needed some work. He said that in recent months the service had deteriorated, and he had to go to a nearby competitor when they needed something in a hurry. This salesman was smart enough to spend the remainder of the day polling his other customers in the area. He found out that their service had deteriorated so badly that many customers were abandoning them. A late-afternoon meeting with his key people determined that they had taken on some businesses in outlying areas and it was keeping their people and trucks tied-up so they couldn't deliver to their already-existing good customers. The end result was that they had to tell some outlying customers they were sorry they couldn't serve them, and re-build their service for the customers that were mainstay. How are you doing with your service? What would your customers really say if an outsider polled them at this very moment?

Epilogue

A lack of complaints doesn't mean your customers are out of ammunition. It may mean they are simply reloading, and they're going to come after you again.

141

Meet Uncle F-E-S-S

You already know that getting new customers takes persistence, hard work, and doing your homework. If you don't anticipate objections, roadblocks, or excuses (and have answers to them), then you're going to be lonelier than the Maytag repairman. The secret is to know in advance what you're going to say and do when a customer presents an objection.

Joe was a real pro at selling training programs and earned a six-figure income because he had answers before the objections came along. He called it his Uncle F-E-S-S, or Frequently Encountered Sales Situations. He anticipated what buyers might use as an excuse not to buy, and could deal with it in advance. For example, when one prospect said he wasn't going to buy Joe's training program because some of his people weren't going to use it, Joe complimented him, and told him he was absolutely correct. However, Joe also said research had proven that some of his salespeople would embrace the training program, have huge sales increases, and make him a lot of money. He was right, and the gentleman signed the purchase order for the training materials, and Joe went to the bank, turning a prospect into a new customer.

Epilogue

Think like a Boy Scout and Be Prepared. Know what you're going to say before you encounter those deadly objections.

142

Don't Be a Drop-in Visitor

Prospects want, need, and will respond to you making them feel valued, respected, and accepted. By telling them you are calling on them because you just happen to be in the area, tells them that you are an accidental tourist without planning or forethought, it destroys your credibility. Always make them feel special because you came just to see them, regardless of how many other people you might see today, or what your plans are.

When Bob, a seasoned insurance company representative, made calls on his prospects, he made them feel so valuable they felt guilty because they didn't buy from him. If he saw only one prospect or 10 in a given day, he had the ability to make them feel like they were the only company Bob visited. What can you do to let prospects know they are the most important person in the world, and that you're coming to see them because you value them?

> **Assignment**
>
> Work at learning what makes prospects feel valued, respected, and accepted, and deliver that to them and watch your new-customer count soar.

Epilogue

Making a prospect feel special, like a rose among the thorns, can have a huge payoff. They will welcome you back gladly.

143

Don't Love Them and Leave Them

His name was John Cash Penney, but you probably know him better by the retail stores he founded, JCPenney. As a retailing pioneer, John Cash Penney believed the best service you could give was the service after the sale. He knew that following up with customers and backing up what you say and do is crucial, because it leads to long-term customer relationships.

John Deere, maker of everything from lawn tractors to combines, launched a new program to sell its expensive high-quality

Assignment

Look at the products and/or services you provide your customers. Which of them would be good as a follow-up relationship building call? Which are most likely to cause problems? Based on the answers to these questions, develop a *service after the sale* program to help you retain those valuable new customers.

lawn tractors. With each purchase, the buyer was promised that after using the lawn tractor a few times, a service technician from John Deere would be out to run a six-point inspection; that they would make absolutely certain it was in perfect working order, that everything was adjusted properly, and they could almost be assured that it will give many years of long-term mowing with little maintenance. This gave John Deere the opportunity to catch a problem before it became a disaster. It was a chance to remind customers that they've invested in a high-quality lawn tractor, and it's a great chance to save a lot of money, because they'll probably prevent some service incidents that would require emergency calls later. What can you do to offer your customers service after the sale so they will look to you for future purchases?

Epilogue

Providing service after the sale works great, because almost nobody does it.

144

Organize Your Prospect Efforts

If you are attempting to organize, track, and cultivate a quantity of prospects, then investing in software specifically designed for managing a database of potential customers may be a great investment for you. It can help you formalize, organize, and systemize your prospecting efforts and offer you reports to show how you are progressing.

Many sales representatives who are drop-dead serious about cultivating new customers have been overwhelmed by the many things a database software program has done for them. You should check out popular brands like ACT, Goldmine, or Microsoft Access, or Microsoft Outlook to understand how you can systemize your contacts. Such automated software gives you great opportunities to do mailing, keep sales call records, as well as the ability to e-mail, fax, and print custom letters to your prospects. If you're trying to manage a quantity of prospects, then a good database software program is a must.

> ### Assignment
> Research the options mentioned at left, select one of the applications, and then build your database of customers. Remember that any database is only valuable if it is kept up-to-date.

Epilogue
The secret of developing new customers is to have a systemized approach to consistently go after those potential customers.

145

The Agony of Defeat

Let's face it: sometimes the work and effort of prospecting and getting new customers is tough. You hear the word "no" again and again. You feel defeated, and everything inside of you wants to quit and walk away. You want to accept defeat, give up, and go home. The answer is not giving into defeat. Instead, have a plan to rebuild your energy and spirit when you feel defeated.

> ### *Assignment*
> Do you have people you can call on who will encourage you? Make a plan that when you feel beat up and ready to quit, you've got somewhere to go, somewhere to renew your energy and spirit. It works for Ed, and it will work for you.

When Ed called on us, he was always an excited, wound up, and ready-to-go salesman. Every one of our people enjoyed seeing him come in, and we worked hard to sell his products. One afternoon, I asked him if he ever got down, discouraged, or defeated. His answer shocked me. He said "Absolutely." My next question was "What do you do when you're in that defeated mode?" His answer was to call on the customers who liked him, supported him, believed in him, and encouraged him. When I asked who those are, he said "One of them is you. When I feel defeated, I call on you and a couple others, and they get me going again. It's my plan to overcome that feeling of defeat."

> ### Epilogue
> *The thrill of victory and the agony of defeat are human feelings. The secret is not what happens, but how you respond to what happens.*

146

It Is Not What Happens To You

When working to win new customers, it is certain you are going to have setbacks, disappointments, and discouragements. The reality of trying to win new customers is that at times you will not succeed. There will be speed bumps and unexpected challenges. Your success in getting new customers is not about what happens to you, your success will be forged by how you respond to what happens to you.

After spending months working to win a new customer's business, you know the devastating feelings and emotions associated with hearing those fateful words "no," "sorry," and "we've gone with someone else." What can you do? You can

> **Assignment**
>
> Write out *Expect the Unexpected* and remember it when dealing with unusual circumstance.

get better or bitter. It is everyone's choice to turn stumbling blocks into stepping-stones by improving your competitive skills. The formula to not let obstacles get you is to expect the unexpected. To use setbacks as a reminder that "no thank you" can be your challenge to use those experiences as a force multiplier. You are a survivor, so pick up the pieces, and go looking for new customers.

> **Epilogue**
> *Great sales people are those who have been knocked down 1,000 times, and gotten up to go 1,001 times.*

147

So You Can't Afford To

Perception is the most important word when you are trying to bring new customers into your business list. You should invest in your image, especially when you are attempting to convince customers that you should be their preferred choice. Business cards, envelopes, brochures, and all printed materials (more than any other single factor) should reflect your value more than the words you use.

> **Assignment**
>
> Make a connection with a graphic designer and/or printing facility that can store and print your materials in small quantities.

Make a decision that you're not going to be an amateur, but that you're going to move up to the professional's level. In today's high-tech world of desktop publishing and instant printing, choose quality over quantity with everything that your customers might see.

Epilogue

When you put your best foot forward to impress a prospect, make sure you are wearing nice shoes.

148

Become an Information Junkie

In today's market, where information is everywhere, it is awfully easy to overlook it. One of the things you can do to endear yourself with prospects and customers is to become a resource of information that interests them. Use your association membership, trade journals, daily newspaper, and mail as a resource center to find things that customers would value. Never assume they saw the information. Because so much comes across their desk, there is no way any one person could keep up with it. A photocopier, a note, and a copy of some strategic information can tell a customer you are really sincere about helping them meet their needs.

My friend Dick has an uncanny ability to find things that interest me. From a postcard while he's traveling, to an article about one of my hobbies, to a prediction about the future, he always seems to stay one step ahead of me. Opening mail from him, or even getting an e-mail, is always exciting, because it

Assignment

Use your association membership, trade journals, and other resources to become an information junkie. Identify those top 10 prospects and the various things you could send to them.

will be something that is targeted just to me. Keep top-of-mind awareness, and build an outpost in your prospect's mind where they see you as someone who is truly tuned in to their needs. In a world that doesn't care, you will be a breath of fresh air.

Epilogue

There is no way to predict when that one item you send to a prospect could be the one that opens the door to all of their business.

149

Obsessed With Reputation

Very few business owners and managers realize the need, the value, and the role of reputation in gaining and retaining customers. The dictionary defines reputation as "The views that are generally held about somebody or something." In other words, when someone thinks about doing business with you, your reputation is going to be a big part of whether they decide to go with you or with someone else.

Take a lesson from the Michelin Tire Company, which over the years has pioneered a reputation as

Assignment

Do you even know what your reputation, or the company's reputation, is in the marketplace? Find out by asking. Then assume that if one person is unhappy, ten more are unhappy but haven't told you. Become someone who is obsessed with protecting and safeguarding his or her reputation.

having the highest quality tires. When their 14 cars (more than half the field) pulled out of the 2005 U.S. Grand Prix in Indianapolis, thousands of people were up in arms that they had been cheated. Almost immediately, Michelin protected their reputation by apologizing to the people who had bought tickets, and spending a reported $10 million to give refunds to those who felt they got a raw deal from Michelin. You can bet that was a painful event for Michelin, but in years to come, they will recover all that money, because they did the right thing to protect their reputation.

Epilogue

It is said that past performance is the best predictor of future performance, and that means your reputation tells a story. If it's good, you'll win customers. If it's tarnished, you're in trouble.

150

Invest In Yourself

Do you take good care of your family, your spouse or significant other, and your parents? Do you support your community, civic organizations, and the important things that take place in your neighborhood? Good for you! You deserve a pat on the back. Now, how about taking care of your self? Isn't it time you invested in your future and your success in dealing with people? Regardless of the product or service you sell, the reality is that you're in the people business, and you just happen to sell the product or service you're dealing with today.

When Jimmy was 19-years-old, he had such a poor self-image that he hated to look at himself in the mirror. He hadn't

Assignment

If you could only take one training program in the rest of your life, there are many good ones out there, but my vote would be to take a Dale Carnegie course. Check them out in your area, because they offer numerous programs on leadership, sales, interpersonal relationships, and a variety of other necessary subjects.

done well in school, was never good at sports, and was always overweight. At age 19 he saw an ad in the paper that said "Develop self-confidence." It was an ad for an inspirational seminar, and he went to listen to a Dale Carnegie course. He was absolutely amazed that in just a few weeks, his investment totally turned his life in a different direction. The Carnegie course gave him the tools he needed to feel good about himself, and to feel good about his ability to deal with other people. Isn't it time you invested in yourself? If you check with most top sales people, they are Dale Carnegie graduates. You should be too.

Epilogue

The author James Allen said, "A man is literally what he thinks." If you think better of yourself, you're going to be more successful.

151

The Value of Persistence

If you ask a customer for their business once, it's very unlikely you'll get a significant percentage to say yes, but as you continue to ask the second, third, and fourth time, the percentage increases dramatically. The fifth time you ask is almost magic. Perhaps it's because the customer realizes your persistence indicates the kind of service you would give them.

One way to win new customers is to let them know that you will play second fiddle to their current supplier. By positioning yourself as the second choice, you have the opportunity to be there when their current supplier makes a blunder. The secret is to be in their face at the point of need, or when they want to make a change. That means being persistent. Keep asking and eventually their supplier will drop the ball and you will get the business. How do we know that? How many times have you dropped the ball?

Assignment

Be persistent. Keep reminding them you are there and available and eventually they will bite. In the meantime, do all the things we have discussed that will keep you at the top of their mind for when the time is right.

Epilogue

The phrase "Out of Sight, Out of Mind" couldn't apply more, so be persistent to win new business.

Index

183

About the Author

When Jerry Wilson began his professional career 25 years ago managing a small auto parts store, it would have been hard to imagine that he would become a world-renowned expert in marketing and develop a new marketing and customer retention philosophy called *Customerology*.

Yet that is just what happened. Jerry grew his small auto parts store into an extremely profitable retail store group that dominated the area in which it was located. Not content with simply increasing sales in his own business, Jerry leveraged and expanded this experience, soon becoming well-known for his retail store operations and sales and management consulting.

Jerry was also the author of the highly acclaimed *Word-of-Mouth Marketing, 138 Quick Ideas to Get More Clients*, and *How To Grow Your Auto Parts Business*, published in numerous languages and distributed internationally. Jerry also authored more than 100 feature articles on customer retention for a variety of association and industry trade journals in both the United States and Canada.

As a result of his experiences, Jerry developed a new "science"—*Customerology*—to aid companies in gaining and retaining satisfied customers. As a consultant, Jerry assisted such companies as Firestone, Merchants Tire, Stanley Publishing, and Ripley's Believe It Or Not, helping them rethink customer philosophies, service strategies, and practices. Jerry also served as executive director for a large state trade association and consulted with business leaders on a national and international level.

For example, in New Zealand, Jerry worked hand-in-hand with management to overhaul Rainbow's End Theme Park after its rescue from bankruptcy. After revamping its customer relations system in accord with Jerry's advice, the theme park realized a 70,000-attendee increase from the previous year—quantifiable success as a result of the tenets of Customerology.

At Merchant's Tire, a 100 plus chain of tire and auto service stores based in Virginia, Jerry assisted management with a campaign to reduce customer complaints. After implementing the Customerology system, the chain saw customer complaints plummet more than 50 percent.

These astounding successes led to numerous speaking engagements for Jerry Wilson. As a professional speaker, Jerry appeared before more than 1,000 groups and traveled to all 50 states, as well as Canada, New Zealand, Indonesia, and South America. His keynote presentations, seminars, and workshops benefited countless companies and organizations worldwide.

Jerry was awarded the Certified Speaking Professional (CSP) designation by the National Speakers Association, a prestigious award given to only 400 speakers worldwide. He served two terms as president of the Indiana chapter of the National Speakers Association and also served as chair of the NSA's CSP Certification Committee.

Jerry was honored by being listed in the *Who's Who Directory of the Midwest* and in the *World Directory of Men of Achievement*.